Daughters of the Most High

Daughters of the Most High

Joyce Carlin

Wipf & Stock
PUBLISHERS
Eugene, Oregon

DAUGHTERS OF THE MOST HIGH

Copyright © 2006 Joyce Carlin. All rights reserved. Except for brief quotations in critical publications or reviews, no part of this book may be reproduced in any manner without prior written permission from the publisher. Write: Permissions, Wipf & Stock, 199 W. 8th Ave., Eugene, OR 97401.

All scripture taken from the HOLY BIBLE, NEW KING JAMES VERSION, Copyright 1982 by Thomas Nelson, Inc.

ISBN: 1-59752-863-3

Manufactured in the U.S.A.

"Joyce Carlin takes you on a sensitive and understanding journey to help you leave behind your painful past and walk forward in God's grace."

—Anne Morey, Director of Women's Ministry,
Faith Community Church, Irvine, California

"Joyce Carlin's life is a wonderful example of keeping one's ear close to the Father's chest to hear His heartbeat. Her compassion for the lost, abused, and hopeless of this world is evident in every area of her work, home, and ministry. She can spot the most hurting, wounded, and impoverished woman and in minutes they know they are loved. Her testimony is a touching example of perseverance and the healing that is available through Jesus Christ! You will be inspired as you learn from this wonderful teacher. Enjoy!"

—Stephanie Lane, Co-founder of Living Worship
Ministries, Corvallis, Montana

"*Daughters of the Most High* is a much needed text for our culture that I look forward to passing on to my clients. Joyce Carlin gently takes you by the hand and walks with you as you face the pain of your earthly father's failures and learn how to turn to your Heavenly Father for hope and healing."

—Joan Lockard, LMHC, and staff member of
Columbia Evangelical Seminary

"When I read *Daughters* for the first time, it was as it was being written. The edits hadn't been done, and there were imperfections in the text. Even then, and every time since, its impact on me was and is, well, cathartic! The writing style is as familiar as a chat with your girlfriend over coffee, yet the message of healing in the Lord goes right to the heart. Stories that I knew, lived, or had heard became more pertinent in my relationship with my Father God, and stories I experienced for the first time in the book gave me more understanding. I haven't always known how God loves me, or that He loves me at all; the Lord has used this book to make those facts very clear. My recommendation? Buy a box of tissues and set aside some time to read this book with your Father God close by. Don't worry. He'll be there!"

—Leslie Ann Smith, Principal of Upper Grades,
St. George Classical Christian School,
Music Ministry, Living Faith Community
Church, and Daughter

Dedicated to

My gentle daughter, Leslie Ann, who with grace and courage triumphed over her childhood disappointments to become a woman of stunning strength and beauty.

Contents

Introduction / 1

Chapter 1
What Is a Father? / 6

Chapter 2
What Is a Daughter? / 50

Chapter 3
Who Is to Blame? / 90

Chapter 4
What Do We Do Now? / 107

Introduction

WHEN I was a little girl, I dreamed of one day having my own family, snugly cuddled together in a great, little cottage with tickly, green grass, clean, adorable children, a strong, loving husband, and sweet, background music underscoring a perfect pot of homemade soup bubbling on the stove. That was forty years ago but, just maybe, some of you are members of a younger generation who take your fantasy with dreams of a career, spotless, beige carpet, a loving husband, and children enjoying dancing lessons while you prepare canapés for your admiring friends. There are as many versions of the "picket fence" utopia as there are little girls. Sadly, those little girls grow up, often through some rocky soil, and life happens. I write for those little girl friends out there whose dreams somehow went awry, who have lost hope, faith, and most of all, the will to reach up again and grasp the brass ring. It is for you, wistful child, to whom I am extending this invitation to settle with your hopes and dreams in a final and glorious resting place.

Because I know there are so many wounded, cynical, and skeptical grown-up girls in this bunch, it is with lots of prayer, much wailing and whining, and a truckload of humility that I ask you to trust me on this journey. That you can find peace in the pages of this book is a gamble. Though, feet firmly planted, I can promise you that you *will* find the peace, joy, and realization of your dreams in the knowledge of who you are in the eyes of an adoring Father who even now waits patiently for you to wander through the garden gate and into His arms.

Sharing the Experience

This book is at best a shared experience. I would like to share my life's experiences with you and, I hope, present your case to your satisfaction. In so doing, it is the desire of my heart to spend some time getting to know you. The part about me that I long to pass along is the story of a girl filled with an aching longing to be cherished, understood, appreciated, and, yes, loved by all of the world. Does that sound familiar? Maybe your desires were more practical or, at least, less unrealistic. Perhaps, you only wanted to be cherished, understood, appreciated, and yes, loved by your family and close friends. The degree to which you desired this exchange is not as important as the fact that you indeed did (and do) desire it. If we are similar in those basic needs, then our time together is going to be worthwhile and wonderful. If you, dear sister, cannot relate, then off to the gym! Leave the broken among us to comfort each other and fly away and be free! If you turn to look back even once though, you had better ditch the cross-trainers, push your little tootsies into your fuzzy slippers, and get real with me. I believe this will be a journey worth taking. Why do I believe, so surely, that you will be glad for this time together? My assured demeanor has nothing to do with what an amazing philosopher, or fantastic teacher, or successful woman I am. In fact, I would like to refer you to my beginning remarks about wailing and whining in the process of the preparation of this book. It was *not* my plan to bring you this story. Even now, as I put pen to paper (or inkjet to paper), I tremble with fear at the awesome responsibility that comes with bringing you this message of hope. From the very day or very second that Jesus came into my life, *my* plan went south! And most always, I thank my gracious God for the frustration. Sadly, often I question whether or not the Lord remembers with whom He is dealing here and (oops) chose the wrong girl for the job. But, I know that after dozens of sleepless nights, hours of listening while aching hearts were poured out to me, years of watching my family members, friends, and sisters-in-the-Lord pine away and waste away in hopelessness and pain, the Creator God of the whole universe kicked me into this project.

It started as a small women's conference in my own little church and has grown into a full-time, all-encompassing ministry. My heart is hostage to this message. The Lord will not seem to let it or me go. My prayer is that you will be healed in His Name, seek His face and Will in your life, and, through this time we spend together, be lifted from your despair or complacency to the life of your dreams. What a task!

How Did We Get Here?

I suppose the best place to start is with some convincing opening arguments. Very well. Did you know that at any given moment about 9.5% or 19 million people suffer from clinical depression? Another 5% of the population experience mild symptoms of being "down in the dumps". At least one in six persons experience a serious or major depressive episode at some point in life. And, each year tens of thousands of depressed people attempt suicide. About thirty thousand succeed.[1]

---

[1] http://www.allaboutdepression.com National Institutes of Health, Publication no. 97-

Introduction

How are you feeling? I think I know you well enough to believe you are feeling great sympathy for those sad statistics but have not yet empathized or placed yourself in that picture. Remember, I know you. You are so busy feeling needed that you ignore your own suffering. Because you are resisting the message, I guess I'll have to get tough and use an example.

In the musical play, *Carousel*, the dubious hero Billy Bigelow sings a big soliloquy upon learning that his long-suffering wife is to give birth to their first child. Billy fantasizes wildly about how incredible it will be to have a son and experience so many wonderful "guy" things together. His ego is comically larger than life as he sings of the strength, height, shared name, and future virility of his son. Suddenly, caught in this fantastic daydream, Billy Bigelow stops dead in his tracks, a look of mild horror on his face as he realizes that his expected infant might indeed be a girl baby and sings: "You can have fun with a son but you gotta be a father to a girl!" If you and I are who I think we are, there is a little sting to that. So to drive that point home, I'll share these next statistics with you: 63% of youth suicides are from fatherless homes, 90% of all homeless and runaway children are from fatherless homes, 85% of all children that exhibit behavioral disorders come from fatherless homes, 80% of all rapists motivated with displaced anger come from fatherless homes, 71% of all high school dropouts come from fatherless homes, 75% of all adolescent patients in chemical abuse centers come from fatherless homes, 70% of juveniles in state-operated institutions come from fatherless homes, and 85% of all youths sitting in prisons grew up in a fatherless home. That translates to mean that children from a fatherless home are 5 times more likely to commit suicide, 32 times more likely to run away, 20 times more likely to have behavioral disorders, 14 times more likely to commit rape, 9 times more likely to drop out of school, 10 times more likely to abuse chemical substances, 9 times more likely to end up in a state-operated institution, and 20 times more likely to end up in prison! But I'm still not talking about you, am I? Do you still feel a burning desire to give all of those lost ones a big, well-adjusted hug? Let's try this: daughters of single parents are 53% more likely to marry as teenagers, 111% more likely to have children as teenagers, 164% more likely to be a single parent, and 92% more likely to divorce if they eventually marry. I need you to stick with me. The questions get harder from this point on.[2]

4266 and 99-3561

[2] U.S. D.H.H.S., Bureau of the Census
Center for Disease Control
Criminal Justice and Behavior, Vol. 14, p. 403-26, 1978
National Principals Association Report on the state of High Schools

Suppose (and bear with me) that the preceding statistics are applicable in a more general sense? I'm sure we can agree that the physical proximity, or lack of it, of our parents has a powerful and profound effect on our lives. But for purposes of clarification and to pique our ability to relate, consider this: How many ways can your father and mother abandon you? Oh-oh. I see you shifting uncomfortably in your chair. I know that you have shed more than one tear for those unfortunate children who are orphaned in both a physical or emotional sense by one or more of their biological parents. I could not begin to address all of the damage done by disappearing mothers, destructive divorces, the un-timely death of a parent, or any number of disasters that are falling upon families every day. This is just a first attempt at sharing the healing gift offered by God. If our time together is worthwhile and you are blessed, we'll go on to future endeavors and cross those many bridges. The focus of this book is on how you, as a precious little daughter, were fathered. That's the subject weighing heavily on my heart and why I write this open letter to you. Just take a deep breath, and we will explore this poorly traveled road. I know that you know this means I'm going to ask more probing questions. That's because I want to get to know you or more honestly I want you to get to know yourself. Okay?

You and Your Father

How about if we begin with a less emotional, intellectual probe? Since we agree that all little girls have dreams, entertain this: Are those little girl dreams affected by the failure of our fathers? Experience has taught us that they are. But, I would ask you to turn the question inward. Have you suffered and struggled with self-doubt, self-destructive behaviors, self-punishment, regrets, poor relationship choices, and crazy and risky behaviors of the sexual, physical or spiritual nature? I am aware that this is tough material. But, hang in there, my special sister. We can't make a thing of beauty without a little pain and, in this case, a few tears. There's hope in "these here pages" and I bless your courage to continue. Just to allow you to catch your breath, let me take the spotlight off of you and take some heat myself.

Rainbows for all of God's Children
U.S. Dept. of Justice, Special Report, Sept. 1988
Texas Dept. of Corrections, 1992
www.fatherhood.org
Whitehead, Barbara, "Dan Quayle Was Right," Atlantic Monthly, Vol. 271, No. 4, April 1993.
www.fathersandfamilies.org

Introduction

As a young teenager, I was always mortified to be picked up by friends at my home. My parents were not extremely weird or even grotesquely dysfunctional, but my father had this one thing he did whenever any of his children left the house. Just when we believed that we had avoided the inevitable, right before we closed the door behind us, he would shout from wherever he was: "Remember who you are!" How embarrassing! How insane! How condescending! *How wise!* How could I misbehave with that kind of pressure hanging over my head? And, how that reminder has followed me through my life and even as I raised my own teenaged daughter.

Who We Are

I tell you this story as a prelude to my next question. If you really understood who you are and what our Father God sees when he looks at you, would you ever again experience depression? Perhaps your parents failed you. Maybe you had a rotten childhood filled with despair and abuses. Possibly, your heart is still aching from being ignored or barely tolerated. I propose that you are suffering from a kind of amnesia. I don't think you know who you are. I don't think you understand what a daughter is. I don't think you understand your Father in Heaven. I don't think you need to submit to the pain anymore. And, I think somewhere, deep inside your wounded heart, you hope and believe Father's words when He said: *"He who has begun a good work in you will be faithful to complete it!* (Phil 1:6b, paraphrased) He wants you to know that . . ." *the temporary sufferings of this world can never compare to the glory that shall be revealed in you."* (Romans 8:18, paraphrased) I am humbled and afraid as we begin this journey. But, come on. I have to do it. Dad said so.

Chapter One

"What Is A Father?"

*For You formed my inward parts;
You covered me in my mother's womb.
I will praise You, for I am fearfully
and wonderfully made . . .*

—Psalm 139: 13-14

WHEN WAS the last time you watched a made-for-TV movie chronicling the joys and struggles of two, sweet expectant parents as they prepared for the arrival of their child? We see these kinds of movies much less than we used to years ago. The more current topics seem to emphasize the breakdown of the family and the horror of alternative lifestyles. Still, I'm sure you can recall at least one story of triumph for the nuclear family, created in the hearts and minds of Americana. Just for nostalgia, focus on that little mommy and daddy as they tick away the months, anxiously filling each day with the wonder and growing love intended by our Creator. I'm sure, if you have ever given birth in a traditional sense, you remember the experiences of carrying, protecting, and delivering your baby. Usually, the discomfort and agony of pregnancy and childbirth quickly give way to the joy and overwhelming love of motherhood. And, the stories of the pain remain just that, stories to tell to others who have been through the same thing or are embarking on the possibility. At any rate, we become mommies from our first realization of the growing person within us. We celebrate each milestone of this special creation and glory in the wonder of movement, warmth, heaviness, and contentment. Perhaps, your time-in-waiting was not so traditional, and you have another story to tell. Please just remember, we are waxing nostalgic here and don't get ahead of me.

The point is that, during the pregnancy, you are the custodial parent. You are the one vomiting, over-eating, craving, visiting the potty constantly, unable to see your feet, swelling, sweating, freezing, crying, screaming, sleeping, and fretting over how you look, how the baby is doing, and what in the world you were thinking getting into this predicament! Daddy is usually just handing out cigars, getting pats on the back, and tiptoeing around you. If you believe that, I've got some property I'd like to discuss with you!

The Beginning of the Journey

Well then, what is a father? Where does fatherhood begin and where should it end? Is there a recipe for being a daddy and, if so, where can we get one? I only bring this up because most of you can't relate to the father of the made-for-TV movie. It's a great story, but it does not make us weep because it is so sweet. We weep because we are in mourning for our own lost father and our own missing joy. What in the world was my dad thinking? And, why does that thought hurt so much? I am aware that these are hard questions. I somewhat apologize for the discomfort, understanding full well what is festering down deep in your soul. I just know that you will be comforted and restored by answering them. You know, it's like when you have a really nasty "owie" that is infected and must be opened, cleaned, and treated in order to heal. It is still up to you whether or not to take this journey. I'm not holding a Twinkie in front of you, demanding that you read or starve. (I just love Twinkies. I know some of you are cupcake girls, and I still love you, but Twinkies—oh my!) As we salivate together, I beg you to muster your strength because I promise, if you take this message to heart, whatever pains you have suffered can heal. This terrible secret may even become your badge of courage. The wrongs can be righted and you can be victorious. *"Oh, victory in Jesus, My Savior, forever."* Remember that old hymn? You know it's true, so just imagine that Jesus is holding your hand even now, staying close by, never to leave. Ask Him to stay and keep reading. This is going to get exciting.

Imagine that you are searching through the classifieds for some exotic, unique job opportunity to replace your current lively occupation. (I'm a big kidder. I hope you will forgive me.)

Clearly, one of the ads sticks out as a point of interest: WANTED: SUPERMAN. (Who doesn't?) Stay in one place most of your life. Do the same things over and over. Worry daily and nightly about finances, home repairs, auto repairs, relationship stresses, large or small parenting mistakes, the safety and physical comfort of your companions and associates, your health, the necessity of pleasing your superiors, your own career goals and frustrations, your inability to perform any one of these tasks, and the constant possibility that it could all be taken away at any moment.

Where do I apply? Right? I'm only partially kidding because these are a few of the general requirements for traditional fatherhood. Of course, the job description gets more detailed depending on each man's individual circumstances. For example, one might also need to be a qualified counselor, a spiritual advisor, a capable and adequate provider, a patient listener, a gentle persuader, a comforter, a teacher, a thoughtful husband and father, a hero and champion, a dreamer and organizer, a plumber, electrician, roofer, carpenter, landscaper, handyman, mechanic, sanitation worker, public speaker, mediator, referee, chief executive officer, accountant, salesman, public relations officer, security guard, romantic, caring and respectful lover, entertainer, chauffer, vacation coordinator, snappy dresser, tidy roommate, disciplinarian and watchful shepherd, affectionate, involved, fine example to all, humble servant, and practical problem resolution technician. Whew! Don't trample the other applicants getting out of here!

Where Do I Turn For Healing?

The point of this flight into fancy is to help bring focus to some of our expectations and those realities that are often forgotten in our times of neediness or sorrow. I'm just asking you to consider that your list of must-be's *might be* a little energetic, at the least. It may even be that you have been brainwashed to a degree by your childish (and often, selfish) desires. Did you want the perfect father? Did you expect humanly impossible behavior? Are you, or someone you know, capable of meeting your model for the perfect father? Have you been a little hard on dear, old dad? Maybe not, since I know that some of you have real and painful wounds that are still healing. Please, do not think that I demean those experiences in any way. Just think about giving your father permission to have failed somewhere—to have been imperfect. Allow yourself to entertain letting him off the hook for his mistakes. You might even try assuming that your father did the best that he could in his circumstance. Not ready for that yet? That's all right. Your father may not deserve this forgiveness. I just know that you do not deserve to carry this tormented aching around in your stomach or neck for even one more precious day. I think it's time for us to take a few moments for a little heart-to-heart between you and me. And, I also know this does not surprise you.

There is a time in the lives of us all when we are largely alone with ourselves. It is certainly not in the bathroom, if you are a mother. That seems to be the time our kids, or that big kid we married, need their socks, something to eat, or for you to count their fingers pushed ceremoniously under the bathroom door, just to keep you in the game. No, I'm speaking about the moments before sleep overtakes you at night. It's a queerly, quiet time when all the others in the home are asleep, including bigfoot who has all the covers. I hope I am not the only freak who stares at the ceiling and counts the triumphs and tragedies of the day at sleepy time. Please, tell me that you spend at least a couple of seconds worrying or awfulizing about future events, past failures, or forgotten details. If not, send a little donation. I need help. But, if you fit this nighttime profile, take a moment to recall those tears and fears. Because this behavior keeps you from resting, it is punishing and destructive. As a little girl, you probably took over this responsibility very early on. After all, when final quiet reigns, who will remind you of your lack of worth if not you? Don't despair. I remember that we are discussing what a father is and not what a mess you are.

Anyway, those final evening thoughts creep into your very soul and keep you from falling into peaceful slumber before snoreman begins the evening performance, right? Or, if you are single, the thoughts keep you up re-reading *Sense and Sensibility*. I know what you're doing. Anything is better than facing true north and having your throat close off painfully, as you fight back tears—again. I'm not asking you to analyze yourself. There are plenty of books out there to help you delay joy, written by many who are much more educated than I in the art of psychology. I will leave that business to them. (Besides, I think they are awake, too!) I just want to share the peace that passes all understanding with you. That doesn't require all those college courses.

I'm going to guess that you spend most nights taking upon yourselves the mantle of the failures of others. That is much less comforting than goose down. I also think that one of the people who failed you was your dad. I told you I'd get back to him. Please accept my invitation to consider that at least some of your sadness, depression, feelings of self-doubt, worthlessness, and the subsequent reflections on poor choices may be tied up with your childhood experiences with him. Little girls have a deep need to be fathered with integrity, gentleness, and reverence. Most of us did not internalize our lives that way.

What Should A Father Be?

So, what should a father be? I am compelled to go to the source of fatherhood and to the manual given us by God. I want you to know that our Father God would share this message with you right this minute. Try very hard to vicariously enjoy this thumbnail portrait and bask in the plan our Father in Heaven has for you.

I began this chapter with the beautiful Psalm 139, in which God reminds us that He has always known you. Not only did He create the heavens and the earth, but also, at just the right time and in just the right place, He created your *"innermost being."* (Psalm 139:13, paraphrased) He took his big, old needles and knit you together in your mother's womb. Can you imagine? You were once a little, tiny body, inside your mommy. Think of it. You were *"carefully and WONDERFULLY made"* (Psalm 139:14, paraphrased) as the precious child of God who planned all your days and thinks of you more times each day than the number of *"grains of sand!"* (Psalm 139:17&18, paraphrased) Daddies should do that. Somewhere along the way, you learned to behave according to some set of human blueprints perpetrated by a mortal and imperfect father and not the high goals of our God.

Did you realize that the Creator of the universe has plans to prosper you and not to harm you? That's what *real* dads think about. Additionally, He wants to give you hope and a future. Romans, chapter 8, says that He will reveal His glory in you. How's that for a Father's pride in his child? I can think of little that is more gratifying than the loving desire of a righteous father to have his baby girl as His representative.

I Am Not Worthy

I'm asking you to give up a lifetime of learned behavior to experience this joy and peace. As miserable as your life may have been, I know how scary that is. By the way, this is about the time that you are arguing with me (or more honestly yourself) about your worthiness to be loved by Our Father in this manner. Surely, I don't understand just how miserable a wretch you are. Certainly, the King of Kings does not desire you in the throne room. After all, what about your sinful past, your filthy habits, your tattered resolves? Imagine if someone you truly loved were to come to you with a broken arm, skinned knee, shameful secret, or damaging confession to name a few, and you blamed and punished and disowned. You wouldn't do that. A good father wouldn't either. He might say something like this, as He did in Romans 8:38:

> Precious child, no matter how high
> you soar or how deep you sink, nothing,
> not even death can separate you from Me
> and My love for you. No demons or powers
> from hell can keep us apart. I will NEVER
> leave you nor reject you. Do not be afraid.

> Do not be dismayed. For, though you walk
> through rivers of pain, the waters will not
> overwhelm you. If you walk through fire,
> you will not be burned. I, the Lord, will be
> with you wherever you go, always. (Isaiah 43:2-5, paraphrased)

Those are big daddy shoes to fill certainly. And, I think a small illustration may clear the way for the possibility.

When I was a little girl of three or four, our family was fortunate enough to own a backyard swimming pool. My father was an excellent swimmer and was occasionally focused on teaching all seven of his children to swim. One thing that I can say about daddy was that he was a good teacher. We were not exposed to any whimsical philosophy that allows dim-witted parents to toss perfectly good kids into the water to just sink or swim. Not all of us just do that naturally. Some of us are terrified and timid and not all that interested in the process. My father was adequately patient and gave helpful advice about kicking and paddling and blowing air from your nose. Still, there came a time when he expected each of us to venture into the water, basically alone, and "swim" several yards (or was it miles?) into his waiting arms. I can't justly explain the thoughts that go through the mind of a three-year-old as she descends into the enveloping water, aching to reach the safety of another's arms. I know that I was panic-stricken, forgot all of the advice, swallowed water, flailed through that liquid grave, a nd came up into dad's arms, coughing and screaming for my more protective mother. My point is that my father was always there. He did not see the need to force me to survive on my own, to tough it out, and push through the fear. He just caught me. That's what good fathers do and that's what little daughters need. Don't forget that dad.

My sister, our Father in Heaven has promised you that He will always be there. Jump in. His arms are strong! No matter how badly your dad blew it, God knew he was going to, watched out for you, carried you through the bad times, wrapped you in His unconditional and all-encompassing love, and pulled you up. He revealed this love through His Son, Christ Jesus, and so in all things and in every situation, you will have that blood-bought victory. Jesus *is* your victory and your Savior sent by Father to catch you when you fall.

A Change of Perspective

I am hoping, at this moment, that you are beginning to experience an attitude change. Do you remember that I suggested that your behavior was learned early on? I know that you have the ability and fortitude to change that behavior if you desire. And, it is that attitude change that will give you your life back. Do you recall the *Sesame Street* song about how your responses depended on "where you put your eyes"? Your perspective determines your response and your beliefs. We're changing beliefs here, so let's take another view.

Sadly, I'm not much for handwork. You know the kind of thing I'm talking about: needlepoint, cross-stitch, crochet, and that stuff. I think my impatience precludes me from handing down these kinds of mementos. If you are talented in this manner, you go girl! But, don't try to get me to do it because my blood pressure is already a borderline event. Meanwhile, I do have a point. Have you ever looked at the back of your embroidered piecework? The front part is a vision of color, design, and geometric beauty. The back part however is a nightmare of knots, strings, and, (in my case) boo-boos. You've probably heard a similar illustration before. I bring it up to open the subject of skeletons. This is not a reference to biology class but your personal closet that may or may not be full of them. We all have them, some little and gruesome, some huge and horrific. Your dad should know about yours. If he doesn't or didn't, your level of communication is questionable. If he does or did know, and it colored your relationship with dishonor, you are not alone. For many of us, those awful monsters are a result of the sins of our fathers and we are not alone.

Now, we all stand in awe of those of you whose father knew about the back of your needlepoint and loved and supported you anyway. Most of us are still hiding our little cotton and polyester monsters. We don't believe that our dads will pick us up, brush off the dirt, put us back on track, and appreciate the right side of our handiwork. We don't believe it because it did not happen that way for us. Probably, your dad was less than the father of your dreams. But, if you could just manage to turn around a bit in your tight, stifling world and glance over your shoulder toward the Father who created the heavens and the earth and yes, YOU, those dreams can come true. Please, do not count on sinful man to lift you up and know your beauty. I'll just ask you to consider letting your earthly father off the hook long enough to get to know Father in Heaven.

He spells it out for the thickheaded among us (that's me) in the beautiful Psalm 139. The message here is that God knows everything (I mean, everything) there is to know about you. He knew us *before* we were born. It was the Creator who placed you lovingly in your mother's womb knowing full well what a disappointment you would be later. He sheltered your tiny body in there forming each precious part and whispering the breath of life into you at the perfect moment. You are *wonderfully* made! He watched over you each and every second, thinking of you constantly. Why would He stop now? Would you? Your Father in Heaven is with you *always*. He doesn't take vacations, or slack off for a few hours a night. He knows ALL about you, loves you anyway, and protects you with a vengeance. The other side of your needlepoint is just the foundation of your beauty to Him.

Have you ever heard that if your past had been different, you would not be who you are, today? I'm not in the business of recommending sin as a rite of passage. It is destructive and to be avoided at all costs. But look, how long will you impede your mission because you live in an imperfect past? Incidentally, it is Satan who wants to keep you there. Don't play into those hands. He's not worthy. And, any father who allowed your mistakes to change or inhibit your relationship is stuck in a darkroom, developing. Turn off the light and let him be. God will sort that out.

God's Promises

Our Father in Heaven says He will never leave you nor reject you. When your parents fail you, He will adopt you, pick you up, hold you in His strong arms and NEVER let you go. Don't confuse this with a belief that God will not discipline those He loves. Just as you might snatch a toddler from oncoming traffic, the Lord will turn you away from a dangerous path and discipline you for your good that you may share in His Holiness. This brings a harvest of righteousness and peace and a lifetime of striving to be in His will.

Now that I have you looking in another direction, is your personal perspective changing? We can see things we have never noticed before from another vantage point and change our future. If you desire healing, you must get on with living. Leg cramps have to be walked off, wounds have to be exposed to the air to knit together, and emotional scars need to be cleansed with the blood of the Savior. The sadness you feel, the self-doubt that cripples you, the regrets that keep you frozen in your tracks are not the result of generational sin. These are learned behaviors and they can be *un-learned*. Job 23:10 says:

> But He knows the way that I take.
> When He has tested me, I will come forth as gold.

Did you hear that? Gold. That's the good news. The bad news is that the refining part hurts. It requires intense heat and long, painful processing. I just want you to be finished and polished and cool down. Rest in the Lord, and He will lift you up.

The Need to Do Something

I always recommend to my sisters in the Lord, as they work through these old wounds, that a time of mourning may be helpful. I look at it this way. *You* didn't make the choices your father made. You certainly would have changed a thing or two (thousand). Still, you are dealing with the pain perpetrated against you because of your father's choices. What if you just let that die and bury it in the backyard of yesterday along with pet rocks and spoolies? (Whew! Am I old or what?) Have a good old wake or dramatic cry, wailing and all, if you like. Or, just sit back and daydream the father you wished you had. Make him amazing in every way and finish it off with a really, gut-wrenching *Love Story*-type ending, where someone gets a terminal illness and passes away in the sweetest farewell scene ever. Or, do what my little, four-year-old daughter used to do with her pretend friends. She would destroy them in the most heinous of accidents. (I often wondered how my sweet, little, angel thought up that stuff.) Then, she would quickly go on to play something more fun. What a great example.

Please. I'm not trying to minimize the heartache of this loss. It's just that I know, as soon as you do this, there is a brighter day. Hello is the mirror image of goodbye. You see, you can't forgive or even hope to love your father until you allow him to be imperfect. It's not you. (REALLY) It's him! Cry it out. Tears are good for the body and the soul. They cleanse and tenderize us. Nothing is as satisfying as the long sigh at the end of a good cry.

What Can Flesh Do?

> Whenever I am afraid,
> I will trust in You.
> In God (I will praise His word).
> In God I have put my trust;
> I will not fear.
> What can flesh do to me? (Psalm 56:3-4)

There it is, the last line of this Psalm, "What can flesh do to me?" Some of you have horror stories to tell that would keep the rest of us up *all* night sympathizing with you. My early childhood was punctuated by an awful reality that was never to be spoken of again in my home. My parents just couldn't face that nightmare with me. The good news (?) is that my father was not the perpetrator. Some of you, my little sisters out there, cannot say the same thing. Even now, as I write these words, I must stop for a few moments, take a deep breath, and feel great sadness for these beautiful, broken hearts. The keys of my computer stand still for a time. I can imagine the cold lack of hope that settles over a child of such treachery, and I do not seek to minimize your pain in any way. But please, just entertain these thoughts for a moment.

The Perfect Sacrifice

If you had a perfect child . . . (Don't even go there. Your kid broke your best dishes, took gum from the store, and didn't wipe off the toilet seat, either!). But, if you *did* have a perfect child like Our Father in Heaven had, you would most likely delight in Him and be filled with greater love than we can understand. We know that Jesus was the spotless Lamb, sent to earth to live the perfect life we could not live, suffer the stunning pain of our sins, and rise again to make clear our way to heaven. We also know that He is loved by the Father beyond our capacity to know. And still, during those awful days at the end of our Lord's life, the God who created the whole universe stood by and let it all happen.

Read that sentence again. Go on. I mean it.

Okay. When you are experiencing a truly awful circumstance and you wonder why, if there really is a God, He does not step in and save you, remember His Son, Jesus. Jesus had no sin in His life. He never hurt anyone, unjustly. He came to seek and save the lost, not to harm little, helpless girls. He was love, and beauty, and hope, incarnate. And, His neighbors beat Him into an unrecognizable figure, spit on Him, nailed Him to a cross, ridiculed His suffering, and reveled in His death. Father did not save Him. He knew something we did not. He knew that ALL things would work together for the good of those who love Him. He knew that the glory to come would be worth the suffering. And, sweet friend, He knew that some day YOU would need a Savior to enable you to go home to Him. Our Father was thinking of you, then. He was with you during the awful times of your life, and He stands by you, now. He said He knew you *before* you were born and predestined you to conform to the likeness of His Son, Jesus Christ. I don't know about you, but I'm not sure I can fill those sandals!

Your destiny and your purpose is to become one with Jesus, share His inheritance, and be with Him in peace and love for all time. And, because of this plan, only Jesus can fulfill your deepest needs and your deepest desires and heal your deepest pain. Your earthly father could not and cannot. Your earthly father will fail by this comparison. Your earthly father needs to be busy working out his own salvation with fear and trembling. Judging by the harm he may have inflicted upon you, I'd tremble too! But, let's just selfishly focus on you, for now.

What Looks Like Love

In the process of continuing our journey through the concept of fatherhood, we need to establish some rules and parameters. This way you will know what you missed, what you may have learned, and what you can teach the father of your children or your grandchildren. Please know that there is no need to perpetuate this misery from generation to generation. You can stop it, now. You have the power. You have the heart. You have the desire, and you have God to lift you up. And, in doing so, your sadness can heal. Remember the old adage: "If life hands you lemons, make lemonade." Well, sister, get out your pitcher because here come a few more recipes!

I'm just wondering, right now, if you can recall a special teacher, friend or acquaintance that affected your life in some way most likely without you or them even knowing it. There is often a great deal of fear and trembling connected with the acknowledgement of this kind of gift. We usually let these experiences go without thanking or telling the person how their kind act or sage advice helped us in a scary time. Anyway, can you think of someone like that in your life? I know I can.

I remember a favorite uncle of mine who would often visit our home to check up on the family or just say howdy. I liked him because he would laugh with a deep, heartfelt sound that must have come from his roots. That is a sound I still remember and cherish. On one of his visits, I had been ill with strep throat for several days, a malady that afflicted my youth over and over. To make this situation worse, it was my birthday. I felt horrible and had been waiting for a phone call from my daddy to wish me "Happy Day". That call never came. Mother explained that she was sure my dad wanted to call but had just been too busy. But, he loves you, she assured me. By this time in my life, I was already wise to that one. I liked her words but was lookin' for some action to back 'em up! We'll talk more later about how not doing what you say can cause terrifically grievous damage.

To continue my story, my loud-laughing uncle stopped by to visit on my special day, noted my sad countenance, came to my bedside, scooped me up, and said some of the most magical words I have ever heard: "Looks like someone needs a big daddy hug!" It was like he read my heart. Boy, did I ever need that hug! Of all the hugs of my life, that one makes the top ten list. I loved that uncle. I think I even appreciate it more today because I understand that he was taking a risk. Strep throat is very contagious, and he just didn't seem to care. Wow! You see, fathers take risks for their cherished little ones often placing themselves in harm's way for the sake of a tiny heart. I learned that from Uncle Marv. I carry that with me today as I serve the little ones in my care.

I could go on with dozens of stories about teachers who changed my life, friends who taught me the real meaning of sacrifice, and a daughter who, with conviction and gentleness, remains faithful to this day to her mother. But, I think you can conjure up your own memories. This is why we are spending this time together. I know you will learn from the nostalgic moment, also. So, go on. Think about it. No, really. Put the book down if you need to and really think about those people with their random acts of kindness that changed your focus or cheered your heart or even saved your life. Then, come back, and we'll move on.

All Is Well

I hope it is obvious that there is a point to this exercise. You see, sister, you are effected by your experiences and Father God is the architect of it all. You would not be who you are without (or sometimes in spite of) your life's experiences, good or bad. And, when it comes time for you to extend the hand of service, it is your life's experience that allows you to sympathize, or advise, or weep in empathy with another wounded soul. Lemons- yes. But, it's not the lemons that make the lemonade. It's you. Perhaps, your father was as inaccessible as mine or was even unwilling to spend time with you. That's not right. I give you permission to be angry and grieved about that. But, at the same time, take to heart this message: The God who created you is MORE than sufficient to supply *all* of your needs. You may have to be creative, yourself, and look for that ordained nurture in safe and unique places, but know that Father has placed it there.

I am reminded of one of my very favorite hymns: "It Is Well With My Soul". Horatio G. Spafford wrote that hymn after losing a fortune in real estate, suffering the terrible loss of his young son to scarlet fever, and the deaths of his four beautiful daughters, victims of a shipwreck. He wrote this hymn about *"peace like a river, sorrows like sea billows"* and great losses such as his own. And, he concluded that *"whatever his lot"*, His Father had taught him to say: *"It is well, it is well with my soul"*.

This earth is not our home and our Eternal Father waits for us to come home to His arms. As James remarked in the New Testament epistle:

> My brethren, count it all joy when you fall into
> various trials, knowing that the testing of your faith

> produces patience. But, let patience have its perfect work, that you may be perfect and complete, lacking nothing. (James 1:2-4)

I believe when the scripture says, "lacking nothing", it means, literally, NO THING. The promise of a faithful Father sure and constant is more than enough. His message is clear:

> Fear not, for I am with you. Be not be dismayed, for I am your God. (Isaiah 41:10)

Can it get any better than that? I'll just fill in the blank for you. Nope.

Turn To God

So, Father God is with you, and He cares about you, and He tests and teaches you through the storms and victories of life. And, He expects that you will return His love in kind, doing unto others and all. But glory be! Father also promises to make you perfect and complete and provide for all of your needs. This promise of completeness includes your need to be loved and nurtured by your dad. This includes your need to be understood and respected. It does not leave out your need to be taught and protected. All of this and more is your promise as you serve, and pray, and study, and keep your focus on Him. I know you have been greatly hurt. I'm asking you to turn to the perfect Father of us all. He loves you. And, the really great news is that He doesn't just provide lip service. He follows through on His promises, blesses your life, and will heal your wounds. Then, go and do thou likewise. It's a kick in the pants. Loving and nurturing someone else is the best antidote for sorrow and pain. I know you can do it. There's a storehouse of love inside of you just waiting to spill over. Let it go. Or, in the words of a modern-day hero: "Let it roll!"

Our Inheritance

Now then, I'm about to encroach on some of that dangerous territory known by all womankind to be highly sensitive. Tell me. Which one of your parents do you LOOK like? Whose nose do you have? Whose eyes? Is you hair color closer to you mother's or your dad's? Come on. When you run into long-lost relatives in the mall, what do they say when they pinch your cheeks into hamburger? Probably, both of your parents are attractive folks. But, whom do you favor? And, does that question cause a little sense of stinging? I think we do not want to act or look like our parents. After all, you are a happening kind of girl—current and hip, right? Right. Looking or acting like our old, stodgy, parents is just too much disappointment. I'm not trying to embarrass or offend you. I'd just like to know more about you and why you hate your ankles. You'll see the point in a moment. Just let me digress for a few. K?

I once met an adorable, little, redheaded girl. She was 4-years-old, chronologically, and about 21-years-old, mentally. I mean, she was precocious, but not in that please-get-this-little-devil-spawn-child-to-go-away kind of way. She was just thoughtful and bright and old beyond her years. Well, I thought she was darling, and I can never resist a cute kid. I love 'em! So, I asked her where she got her beautiful, red hair. She quickly answered: "From my rusty, old parents." Obviously, she had been coached, but I laughed anyway, because that's funny. She knew it was funny and laughed along with me. It was a delightful moment that just happens to illustrate what I'm talking about. I know this comes as little surprise to you.

In The Image of God

Did you know that you are created in the image of your Father? Yes, I mean you. The female child of God often misinterprets how she could possibly be created in His image. If you study the Bible, you know that God is Spirit and certainly not limited by our finite mind to a male persona or body. Then what does this mean when Father says we are created in His image? All are created in the image of God and display His attributes in some form or another. Those of us who are redeemed have the ability to reflect His image on a much greater level. Now, I don't know about you, but I have not been feeling particularly superhuman or extra-terrestrial. It's not really that lofty of a concept. God has real and constant character traits that comprise a part of our inheritance. He has bequeathed them to us. If you call Jesus your Lord and Savior, you are a joint-heir. Therefore, you are like your Father. But, just what does that mean? Logically, a great first step would be to find out who *He* is and then play the match game. So, here are a few possible character traits to consider.

God's Faithfulness

God is faithful. He watches us continually and without fail. He does not take a break or doze off. He does not get distracted or bored. He keeps track of the hairs on your head and the moaning of your heart. He knows when your tummy or head aches. And, He heals your ills from the heavenlies, even protecting you from those dangers and harmful moments that you did not see coming. God did, and He wrapped you in His care. So, Father asks you to be faithful. It's the least you can do and one of the hardest tasks to accomplish. But still, you are made in His image, and it must be possible. If your earthly father was not faithful to you or to your mother or his duty or on and on ad nauseum, replace that old memory with this perfect Father and "go and do thou likewise."

I may be assuming that you are like me, and the task of being 100% faithful looms as a high hurdle. If you *have* been a perfectly faithful person, I admire you. If you have not, I relate, and so, perhaps, can your father of flesh. Are you able to give him the benefit of the doubt as a beginning step to your own sanctification? This does not mean that all must be immediately forgiven and the relationship is whole. This step of faith only means that you are willing to see things differently. It is a piece of information that may empower your journey, okay?

God's Loyalty

I would be remiss if I did not consider God's loyalty at this point in our discussion. If you *are* anything like me, you have experienced the opposite of loyalty, repeatedly, in many relationships. If not with your father, then a friend, associate, co-worker, fellow student, etc. When you are a tenderhearted and long-suffering personality, you are a perfect target for abuse and betrayal. Possibly, your father set you up for this. Often, the tendency is to marry someone who is both emotionally unavailable, disloyal and *just* like our fathers.

There might be another key figure adding fuel to this fire. I'm not letting those abandoning mothers off the hook. It's just that this is a book about your life with father. Certainly, the emotionally and physically unavailable mother can wreck havoc in the life and growth of a delicate, little psyche. That subject would be best covered in its own volume, so I will delay that discussion and continue to explore our relationship with God.

Your Father in Heaven is impeccably loyal. Once you are His child, He will never let you go. He *cannot* and *will not*. I can only compare this with real life experiences that have impacted my own life, even though the comparisons pale. But just for reflection sake, I share the next story.

My family had the blessed opportunity to reach out a hand of fellowship to a little family in terrible crisis. The mother and father had been flirting with disaster in the form of an evil addiction to drugs. Unfortunately, they had dragged their innocent children with them into despair. To shorten the story, they ran from the law in Nevada to our hometown in St. George,

Utah, and were finally caught and brought into custody. The real victims of this young couple's choices were their children, too young to understand and too wounded to take care of themselves, who were nestled in the back of the get-away van. The three, terrified children were ushered off to a far away state to live with the maternal grandfather, seemingly on a permanent basis. The one child not yet accounted for, was still unborn. This beautiful angel was born in the midst of jail sentences and drug withdrawals. It was then that we came into the picture. God was merciful and these mixed-up parents received grace in the form of a prison ministry whose teachings brought them to the foot of the cross. This was the first time I had ever seen hardened drug addicts give up their drugs and change their lives, literally overnight. Only Jesus can work such a miracle. I apologize to all of my twelve-step friends, out there. I praise God that this method is helping you to heal. But, only the sovereign Creator of the universe can work a miracle this quickly and this completely. To my knowledge, the two have never again touched drugs or fallen back since that salvation moment.

Anyway, I told you that my family had a part in this miracle. In retrospect, the miracle happened to us. No. We were not that little family. But, the precious angel born in this horrific time of trouble was in need of daily care while her parents got it together. That's where we got involved. We cared for this little one from the time she was 3 months old to just after her fourth birthday. She became a part of the family just as integral as my natural daughter. We showered her with love and were loved right back with a passion.

As her parents became more viable, we still shared time with our beloved goddaughter, often. Then, the little family decided to travel across the country to make their home, taking a part of our hearts with them. It was no less painful than if she had been our own. The commitment we had made to their family did not change for us, and the overpowering love we felt for that little one never grows cold. It is a pain and a loss that we cannot overcome and is with us always.

And, I tell you all of this to illustrate how much our Father is dedicated to His children. If the precious baby that we helped raise should return home to St. George, I would never stop hugging her. The thought of holding her in my arms again is a sweet pain that I live with daily. Because of this experience, I can relate to a Father who will never let YOU go. Trust Him. He will stand by you always no matter where you are or what mistakes you may make. And, like the father of the prodigal son, He will never stop kissing you when you come home. You are loved that much by a loyal father in whose character is not one drop of betrayal.

God's Love

Maybe faithfulness and loyalty is something you are still working on. Let's look at another character trait Father passes along to you—love. We like this one. We also hear about this one most often from the pulpit and from each other. Even those who do not seek to do God's Will remind us that God is love, and we should extend that to everyone, no matter upon which platform they stand. These folks don't understand Father's love. Actually, they don't really want it either because it comes with great responsibility. I wonder if your father was one of these types. You know. You *have to* love me. I'm your father. You may add any verb in place of the word, love like respect, or care for, or listen to, or obey. It really doesn't matter. Your dad did not understand a true father's love and commitment, anyway. Because with God's love comes a covenant. That is a powerful word. The closest I can come to a synonym for covenant is mutual obligation. (See? It even takes me two words to equal one of Father's.) When our Father uses the term covenant, He intends that there be an exchange. Yes, He loves all of His children, all of the time. Yes, He loves with a deepness and purity unmatched. And yes, His love is eternal and unchanging. But, did you catch the part about HIS children? H-m-m-m. Perhaps not every one is His child. Think about it. Now, check yourself. Do you desire on any level to have fellowship with the Creator God? Do you long for the rest in the Lord promised when we reach our Heavenly home? Do you cry out to God in times of need and rely solely upon His sovereign intervention? Do you look forward to a day when you will be without sin? Then you are probably His. Those who don't—aren't.

Undeserved Grace

Before we go on, you should know that not all of God's promises are conditional. The problem with many of us today is that we have an attitude of entitlement. We believe that we should be blessed because we draw breath and take up space. So, I hesitate to open the topic of unconditional love because I think I am speaking to the choir, here. Most daughters of extreme circumstances believe that they are not entitled to anything. We think we are the runt of the litter, the dregs of the world, the drones— okay, now I'm getting depressed! (Just kidding.) Anyway, God often blesses His children for no apparent reason because it pleases Him and serves His purpose. We all receive blessings we do not deserve--the gift of grace pops into my mind.

For by grace you have been saved, through faith, and that not of yourselves. (Ephesians 2:8)

These are the things for which in gratitude we should never leave our knees. We'll cover this concept more in a few pages. Let's just focus on our covenantal promise of God's love.

So if you are like your Father in Heaven, you are a lover. Many things bring you to tears. Your compassion gets the best of you in all situations. You desire to help and to right all of the world's wrongs. You put band-aids on a small child's boo-boo. And, you have a tiny bit of regret when you step on a bug. (It may be *really* tiny.) Still, you have a loving and tender heart. That's the same heart that may have been trampled with impunity by a dad with "no respect". He can't supply this need. You did not get your loving heart from him. God, the Father, gave it to you. He said, *"I created you in My image so that you and I can express love to each other. Our relationship is the most intimate of all because you and I are becoming one, you in Me, and Me in you, unified by my love for you. Because you seek to know me, I satisfy your heart with love and joy and the peace that only I can give, and that, you cannot understand."* (John 17:22-23, Phil. 4:7, Col 3:10, all paraphrased) Awesome!!

What Is Compassion?

Did you know that it is His pleasure to show forth loving compassion? It's in the Book. He has compassion on the poor and needy, is the Father to the fatherless (could that in some way be you?), and lifts the downtrodden among us from the depths of despair to set them among princes. Our Father God wants us to do these things also. He is love, and when you live in love, you live in Him. He has shown us what is good, and what He requires of us. He wants us to live justly, to love mercy, and to walk humbly with Him. Just for a moment, imagine walking with this Father hand-in-hand in the cool of the evening. Close your eyes and drink that picture in because this is where you are even now.

Stay with Him. I can wait.

The Law as Love

As we continue, I haven't forgotten that I used the word covenant in this instance. In fact, God says that His love is with those who fear Him and His righteousness is with your children's children, with those who keep His covenant and remember to obey His laws. You see, *His law is love.*

> You shall love the Lord your God with all your heart, with all your soul and with all your mind. This is the first great commandment. And the second is like it: You shall love your neighbor as yourself. (Matt. 22:37-39)

He continues to clarify our portion of the covenant by adding that on these two commandments all of His laws are based. When you walk in love, you are obeying all His laws. When you walk in Love, you are walking in HIS Holy Spirit for GOD IS LOVE! I think you might have inherited this gift from your true Father. I guess we all have some work to do.

To sum up, as an infant we require love in order to survive. This has been proven time and time again, in study after study, in which love is withheld for research purposes, and collected data from case studies supports the thesis. As a growing child, we need love in order to grow into emotionally, physically, and spiritually healthy persons. As a teen, we test love in order to assure ourselves that it will always be available. And as an adult, we seek love to nurture and complete our lives. We need it. Father gives it. Your dad may have been unable or unwilling to give it. At whatever juncture you missed out on being loved, that defining moment colored your perspective and your future. You must reclaim it and focus on the beauty of the needlepoint again. Your Father in Heaven loves you *because* you are His child. It is time to love Him now because He *first* loved you.

The Mercy That Saves

So what about mercy? Of course, that is also a part of God's character and, therefore, may be passed down to the heirs. Mercy differs from grace in that grace is undeserved credit. Mercy is deliverance from *deserved* consequences. Ever been there? I have, and you know there is a story coming.

I was foolish enough to squander my youth and miss out on a college education fresh out of high school. My parents tried to give me direction and even sent me to the University after graduation. I majored in coffee and partying. My real classes suffered. I did not care. However, I cared plenty when at the tender age of thirty-five, I went back to school to get a teaching degree. I had a young daughter and a household to run. How much more pleasant it would have been to accomplish this task in my carefree days. But, I had low self esteem and even lower expectations. I know you understand that. Still, I found myself in classes with perky, young adults (no comment), but this time with a real desire to learn and accomplish goals.

In one particular class, I was required to memorize a great deal of information. Brain cells were dropping like flies, daily, and it wasn't long before I was on overload without enough random access memory to see me through. Here comes the illustration of mercy. I was taking a final exam in American Government that was presented in essay format. We were to be graded on our thorough coverage of the subject. I had studied with a vengeance for weeks and considered myself to be so ready. And then, you guessed it. The professor passed out the test booklets and uncovered the essay questions. My mind went totally blank! Every word I had memorized was gone. I mean, really gone. I could not remember a thing. I sat with glazed eyes for what must have been twenty minutes, real panic setting in like a death sentence. And then, for no apparent reason, the professor called me into the hallway. "What is the problem?" he asked. "You look like you have seen a ghost." I explained that I was experiencing a true "senior" moment and had forgotten every detail of the material. That was the moment that mercy was applied to my education. My professor asked a few probing questions, gave me some minute hints and the information came flooding back. I got an A in the class. My essay answers were some of the best he had ever read! I didn't deserve mercy, but he gave it anyway.

I could go on all day about times I deserved a spanking and one never came, or times I should have been in a twisted heap for driving in an impaired condition and made it home safely, or times my sweet husband should have said: "I told you so" and didn't. That's mercy. And, who is the author of all mercy? Yep. You guessed that too. Our Father God invented mercy. Don't test Him. He knows how to use it!

Mercy and the Heart of God

In fact, if you need to see the Lord in action, just flip over to any of the passages in the Psalms. Now, I had never been much of a fan of King David before doing this. In his life, he fell into the very sins that had visited and re-visited my life from my early childhood into my early forties when I finally said ENOUGH and left a really abusive marriage. Seems like David just could not keep his priorities straight, had a jaundiced and wandering eye, and was not above harming another human being to get what he wanted. That God kept referring to David as "a man after His own heart" really rankled me! I would often try to read a Psalm or two, close the Book and throw things about the room in displaced anger. In hindsight, it may have been therapeutic to toss those things instead of pummeling the men in my life who just kept disappointing me. I learned later that those very men were living their own private hell anyway and did not need my help to be miserable. Many of them had made an art of destroying their own happiness and success.

So, returning to the story of David—what did God mean when he referred to David in such endearing terms? Why should you or I care? I'm sure you know by now that I am going to tell you. Or perhaps, it would be better to let David tell you. Step into his heart and see if you don't recognize the tune.

> Have mercy upon me, O LORD, for I am in trouble; mine eye is consumed with grief, yes, my soul and my belly. For my life is spent with grief, and my years with sighing; my strength faileth because of my iniquity, and my bones are consumed. (Psalm 31:9-10)

Ouch! Many times I lay, with my face in the carpet (at least I had carpet), absolutely writhing in pain with the same prayer on my lips. I wanted mercy. I wanted deliverance. I wanted peace. It was a long time coming.

Mercy to Forgive

However, it is the very recollection of these times in my life that allows me to forgive and understand David. He must have suffered greatly. And, it is always most painful when suffering is at your own hand. If you keep reading in the book of Psalm, you will discover many passages in which David demeans himself and begs for God's forgiveness. But, you will also read much of David's worship of His Father and Ours, and his humble gratitude to a God who forgave, seemingly ad infinitum, someone who certainly did not deserve it. That is Godly mercy. That is part of your inheritance. That is worth its weight in gold. And, that is why I can now forgive David (like it is my place!) and believe that Father will treat me with the same tenderness and patience. I'm just going to entreat you to be merciful. Grant mercy where mercy may apply as God's grace is given. You know when that is because God's Word directs us: *"that through the mercy shown you, they also may obtain mercy."* (Romans 11:31b) Please don't think that I mean for you to be merciful to those really evil-to-the-core people out there. Get help and claw your way to safety. But, if your dad was like mine and just not your perfect vision, grant mercy. It won't hurt you. In fact, it will bring solace and relief. Our Father in Heaven says that vengeance is for Him, not us. Be faithful and stand down. God will exact retribution from those who have harmed you. You know what happened to Korah when he mumbled against Moses. He got his. So, let go and let God.

A Reasonable Faith

What else is within the constant character of God? I am compelled to point out that God is reason. Not that God has His reasons. He does, but that's not what I mean. Just bear with me because most girls don't relate to this trait. We are not always governed by reason. Our emotions loom larger as we navigate through our day. It is certainly not that reason is a greater denominator than feelings. They are both useful in the right moments and in the right circumstances. For instance, I don't want you to calculate the distance between you and an attacker so that you can determine when to run. I want you to trust that good old "fight or flight" hormone and beat feet. Even Chuck Norris (who I think is really cute) knows when to run. I'm talking about your inherited ability to make sense out of the world and false information by using your powers of reason. As a little girl, I was often in a crazy-making tailspin when my grown-ups said one thing and did just the opposite. I still cannot laugh when someone says: "Do as I say, not as I do." I told you I would get back to this one.

If you were ever in an intimate relationship and the words said "I love you" but the actions said "I'm a liar", then you can appreciate the damage done. If you are currently parenting impressionable little ones, please do not do this. I know you know. I just feel so panic-stricken to think of the possibility of repeating the terrible "sins of the fathers". It is not your fault that, as a little girl, you were fooled. You see, our powers of reasoning grow as we learn to make sense of our environment and condition. When you were a baby, one of the first things you internalized was that when you perform a certain action there is often a predictable result. We call this concept cause and effect. I cry. Mom comes running. I hit the button on the toy. Music plays. And with lots of practice and the very predictable outcomes, we learn to reason about probability and control. That makes a happy child. Even more comforting is the knowledge that it is your ability to reason that can protect you from this do-as-I-say trick, now.

The most important thing to understand about this key issue is that reason must be founded on fact or truth. If outcomes are relative or subjective, they are not reasonable. A child must be able to expect the same outcome *every* time he or she performs a behavior. Keep that in mind when you are disciplining children. Consistency makes sense. Inconsistency makes us crazy.

A Consistent God

Our Father in Heaven has an inviolate set of rules that govern His behavior. He *never* changes. But even greater than that assurance is the fact that reason cannot exist outside of God. There is no concept or salient thought that can exist outside of the reason of God. Logic fails. Philosophy fails. Science fails. Psychology fails. Mathematics fails. Even theology fails without the Creator of the universe at its foundation. That's a big subject. Lots of books have been written to explore it. Get one and grow in wisdom.

There is a real healing that can occur when you know that there really is a true north. All things must respond to the commands of Our Sovereign Father. He is the cause of *all* effect. Therefore, you can trust that any action on your part will result in the same outcome *always*. God lives by these rules. If you serve Him, He will bless you. If you follow Him, you will find transcendent joy. If you believe on Him, you will be saved.

The father of your youth most likely was not consistent and did not rely so much on being reasonable as being self-serving. Basically, he was not very smart. He will produce predictable results one day. Don't look back because you can look forward and adjust your responses to produce joy, love, and godly service today. Good advice comes from following God's Word. He inspires others so that good advice may show up in lots of places. I like how Thumper said it in Bambi, "If you can't say somethin' nice, don't say nothin' at all." See? That's good advice. Stand on reasonable ground and speak truth.

So thus far, we have discussed only a few of the traits of God. Remember, that I mean this to be a prototype for fatherhood. I know it is a tall order, but we all need to aspire to something. Daddies should aspire to this, understanding that this is just the tip of the iceberg. We have covered faithfulness and loyalty, grace, love, mercy, and reason. Even if this were all there were, it would be a staggering gift. As Shirley Temple said in one of her many, adorable movies: "I know more!"

The Same Yesterday, Today, and Always

Do you know anyone who makes promises they do not keep, arrives late to every event, changes their story for convenience, or is in such a state of personal flux that it is impossible to predict their behavior, *ever?* I do. And, I'm not talking about how your husband or children *hate* Diet Coke until it is the only thing in the house and then suddenly develop an appreciation for this magic elixir. We find ourselves wishing for one thing that can be considered our special treat that no one else likes. Right now, I'm trying to develop a fondness for fruitcake. That'll show 'em! The point is that predictability and consistent behavior are the very foundation of trust and faithfulness. Unable to count on those things, we become confused and at the pinnacle of the confusion feel crazy as we talk ourselves out of and into endless rationalizations.

Just for the record, we all change our minds and our tastes from time to time. I'm guilty. But, the folks I'm referring to are those people who are never predictable, never consistent, and therefore, never trustworthy. I like to know what to expect from my friends and associates. Don't you? Otherwise, we are just pinball players being pushed to and fro through a treacherous path, unable to achieve success.

Unpredictable Events

Our fathers treated many of us this way. Their moods would change seemingly with the wind so that one time we were his darling, talented daughter and the next the worst thing that ever happened to him. In fact, one of my most bittersweet childhood memories is attached to a wonderful talent given me by my Father in Heaven. I was gifted with the ability to make music with my voice to the delight of many and varied listeners. It was a source of a celebration of joy for me also. How I love to sing! The bitterness of my memory stems from a father who truly believed children should be seen and not heard unless given special audience by an adult. Sometimes, I was given audience and other times not. Now, I know that kids can be very distracting, to say the least. But, when a genuine feeling of mutual respect is fostered between parent and child, discipline becomes gentle and easily accepted. A secure child can sit in on almost any event with quiet and well-mannered ease. Dad did not see it that way. So, I became jumpy and fearful and unable to determine when my presence was acceptable and when it was not. There was a marked effect on my personality, also.

In some circumstances, like with telephone messages, I was expected to be like him. I was supposed to answer questions *his* way and according to *his* timing. Often, all of his children would be instructed (nay, threatened) not to say the wrong thing to the wrong person or give out any extra information. That is a tall order for a child who may not yet understand a daddy who is "not here" when the child can perfectly well see that he is! This type of intimidation permeated much of my early relationship with my dad. I was afraid often of doing or saying the wrong thing. I began to question what I *saw* and began to believe timidly what I *heard*. There's a nice paycheck for some future therapist!

Useful But Not Required

To drive home the point, it was once in a while expedient and beneficial for my father to dress me up in pretty clothes and parade me in front of guests to perch at the piano, play my little songs, and impress the crowd with my vocal talent. They loved it and dad used it to his advantage. I was expected to leave as quietly and quickly as possible after my kind and respectful acceptance of praise. Perhaps, this was my first conscious acknowledgement of being useful but not required. It played destructively on every relationship I had from that point on. I don't think my father knew this. Take a lesson, dads!

Please, do not get the idea that my father was some dark, manipulative man. He was not. He was one of my biggest fans, and loved to hear me sing. In fact, my sweetest memories of him happened at his deathbed as I sang favorite hymn after hymn, held his hand, and prayed for his safe return to the Lord. I could not have loved him more. Our Father in Heaven can heal all wounds and make bad experiences fade to black.

Let Go And Let God

You may or may not be struggling with this type of self-doubt. I hope not. Yet, I think that my story may have struck a chord for all little girls who felt conditional and transient love in those vital, formative years. The awesome Father of this universe knows, cares, and wants to take the scars away. The father of your youth may never be able to right these wrongs. I suggest a little bent-knee therapy. Tell God how badly these things hurt you. Beg for healing. Cleanse your spirit with holy tears and give it to Father. Nothing is too hard for the Lord. Let go. *Let go.* Let God. That's step one. And, as you have come to expect, here comes step two.

The Lasting Effects of Inconsistency

Have you considered how these emotional scars may have colored other relationships in your life? Do you feel familiar pangs in other circumstances with other men? Are you carrying extra baggage into your interactions with others that may need to be un-packed? Don't even mention how this behavior may have wormed its way into your habits. Okay. Let's go ahead and mention it. Did inconsistency impact you with such power that you are not a trustworthy person? Now that you know, you can fix it. I know that your real fear is that if you begin to make promises and follow through, you will be expected to perform this way forever. And, of course, you are an unworthy person and do not want the responsibility that comes with following through. I'm trying to be gentle, here.

Still, may I point out that your father may share these personal doubts. However, he continues to duck and bob his way through life. How long will you settle for such an unfulfilling life? I think today is a great day to make a new resolve. Your family will respect and love you for it. You said you wanted that. If this is not enough incentive, then look at what else God has passed down to you as an inheritance.

Absolute Consistency

Do you remember that after the time of Malachi the canonical prophecies of the Old Testament ceased? The inter-testamental period brought a four-hundred-year silence that I imagine rested very heavily on the children of God. They had become used to an active exchange between heaven and earth through His servants, the Prophets. They had seen signs and wonders. Many miracles had been experienced. And now, suddenly and without much warning, God was silent. Did you know that He did not leave us without comfort? Malachi 3:6 reminds us:

> I am the Lord. I do not change.

How wise our Father is! He assured us of His consistency *before* the long time of waiting. It is much less frightening to wait when you know with assurance the time will pass and all will be well again. How about this one?

> Jesus Christ is the same yesterday, today, and forever. (Hebrews 13:8)

There's consistency for you. The Lord will *never* change. How do we know? First and most important, He said so. But also, our confidence comes from the knowledge that He has not changed yet. He has established a record of trustworthiness. In 55 years, I have not known the Lord to abandon me. I have always had food to eat, clothes to wear, and a roof over my head. He doesn't change. He is always on time. He has been predictable in all circumstances. He continues to keep His word. I can count on God. So can you.

Perfect Faith Casts Out Doubt

I think the book of Proverbs was given as a kind of owner's manual for our use while in this earthly skin. There is a literal wellspring of advice contained in it to point us toward a fulfilled and successful life. Anyway, I'm about to digress again for purposes of clarification. Yikes!

Do you remember your first crush on a real boy? I'm not talking about those poster boys you had pasted all over your bedroom walls. Those guys just provided youthful and momentary lapses into despair. How we loved the catharsis of un-requited love! But then, along came that first real boy. Maybe, you sat next to him in science class. I met mine at a church youth party. O-o-o, I thought I would just swoon right to death! I remember saying something like: "I shall love him with all of my heart—forever!" As it turns out, forever was about 2 months of summer vacation and all of my heart turned out to mean for the moment. I hope you can relate. Otherwise, I look a little silly right now, though it would not be the first time. And, by now you realize that I have an ulterior motive in the telling. I just wanted you to have a baseline understanding for how puny we are in relation to our Father in Heaven. Here's what He has to tell you when you experience doubts:

> Trust in the Lord with *all* your heart,
> And lean *not* on your own understanding;
> In all your ways acknowledge Him,
> And He *shall* direct your paths. *(*Proverbs 3:5-6, emphasis added)

God Will Not Fail

If you are still confused, I mean to change that. Unlike those empty words uttered at the advent of your first crush, God means for you to trust Him with your *whole* heart. (Really) He's not kidding around here. Remember, I said He is impeccably consistent and faithful. He alone deserves your trust and, for that matter, your whole heart. I love the Psalm that compares those who trust the Lord to a mountain. And, the comparison is made not to just any mountain. The psalmist refers to the temple mount of Mount Zion. He says:

> Those who trust in the Lord
> Are like Mount Zion,
> Which cannot be moved, but abides forever.
> As the mountains surround Jerusalem,
> So the Lord surrounds His people
> From this time forth and forever. (Psalm 125:1-2)

He's not going anywhere, soon. He's hanging around well past summer vacation. So, sister, have faith in the Most Faithful. The proof of His faithfulness is your very existence today. Bill Cosby once quipped, when speaking about his children, "I brought you into the world, and I can take you out!" The Creator God of the universe really can. Instead, He continues to provide food, clothing, housing, fellowship, and anything else you need. If you can't see it, you are not looking. The evidence is everywhere. The mountain cannot be moved. Quit trying to move it and have faith. For after all, it is the *substance* of things hoped for and the *evidence* of things not seen. Go ahead and give a big sigh. It feels great!

Though it is my hope that the reality of God's consistency will have a profound effect on your heart, there is much more territory to cross. So, within the framework of learning about and understanding God's character, we must move on to the next aspect.

God as the Source of All Power and Protection

I work often with very young children who in comparison to adults are able to accomplish only tiny tasks. Children who grow up in a physically and emotionally unsafe environment are aware of their vulnerability and are often fearful. These kids ache for any feeling of strength or power and long for protection. We learn early on that might often makes right or, at the least, an inevitable consequence. So, we seek out bigger people to become our champions. A little girl wants nothing more than a father who will protect her and champion her causes. Given a really threatening situation, she can be heard to say: "My dad's bigger than yours!" or "My dad will beat you up for that!" or, how about: "Wait 'til I tell my dad about this!" I imagine that you remember fantasies of a father who would come swooping down to save you in a time of dire need and whisk you off in his comforting arms. Probably in your fantasy, he was fighting the bad guys with his free hand as you both rode off (or ran off) to safety. Every child dreams about this. You are not alone. I further imagine that your dad may not have received the script in enough time to complete the rescue. Maybe, you can sympathize with those of us who not only were not protected in stressful times but experienced betrayal in the form of treachery. I was told that grown-ups were right, no matter what. When my life was inalterably changed at the tender age of five, I was told that I had imagined the abuse. If I complained about a teacher or adult acquaintance, I was invited to find something good about them and stuff my instinctive or hurt feelings. My father seldom gave credibility to my fears or feelings. In fact, his favorite explanatory adjective for my responses was "stupid". It still hurts to think it. Also, if anyone says that to me today, I become unpredictably wacky. I am a work in progress.

Nonetheless, when Beaver Cleaver said, "My dad's bigger than your dad!" our little hearts started pitty-patting and we knew that his father would save the day. I decided then that if I ever had a child, I would protect that child at all costs. I kept my word, too. In fact, I was so protective of my daughter that in the third grade she cried when I could not accompany her on her first bus ride to school. Don't bother with the lecture. I learned something that day and backed off. Now at the tender age of 35, she is protecting me. All aboard the full circle express!

Simply put, a child needs to feel safe and protected. A child needs some control and power over their environment, but someone bigger must provide what a little one cannot. A good father earns the title, protector. He watches and waits and holds his breath in anticipation when his child tries something on his own. And, he catches you in the swimming pool, and steps between you and a bully, and intervenes with your teachers when they are unreasonable. A good father gives you a sense of power as well as a powerful sense of protection. Didn't happen to you? Trust me. I really do feel your pain. But, guess what I have?—a message from Father.

What about Corrupt Power?

First of all, let us delineate between personal power and unrighteous dominion. Most children who are wounded by their responses to childhood experiences cannot differentiate between these two concepts. We have a genuine lack of understanding about power and its characteristics. Since we felt the lack of it, those who had it struck fear in our hearts.

There is nothing more horrific than an inability to escape a physical or emotional attack. I remember having dreams about running from an attacker, reaching my house or car, only to be unable to get the key in the lock fast enough to save myself. Sadly, some of you have true-life experiences like this. If you do not hear any other message in this book, please hear this: What happened to you was not right or righteous. It was the result of sin and evil. You are a victim and you deserve protection.

God's Perfect Power

The truth is that real power comes with great responsibility. If power is not balanced with thoughtful and righteous responsibility, it is called aggression. This alone lowers the perpetrator to the level of a bully, at the least. No one likes a bully. So, you are not alone in your distaste for whoever tormented you. And, if that tormentor was your father, it is a miracle that you are able to lift your pretty head from your pillow each day and leave

What Is a Father?

the safety of your home. It is time to take back your power and to invest your trust in the trustworthy Creator of all that is. You see, Our Father in Heaven is omnipotent. That word means *all-powerful*. He can, basically, do *anything He wants*. Therefore, it follows that everything God wants to happen, *does*. Here we go, raising again the question about the meaning of evil in the world. What always strikes me in this particular exchange is the absence of any inquiry about the meaning of good in the world. But, this is not our subject. Much has been written about this controversy. I'll let you pursue the study another time. I just want to make the point that when God does something, He sticks around to follow through. He *only* acts within His nature that we know now never changes. So, He takes full responsibility for His actions. And, He has done some really great things for you. I know you realize it in your more peaceful times. And, I bet you can relate to one of my now favorite Bible characters, King David. Hold on. I know he causes animated discussions at Wednesday night studies. Remember, we are on a journey into peace. Certainly, King David is the poster boy for that journey.

How God Protects You

Psalm 18 contains some of David's most beautiful and comforting images. I wouldn't mind if you stopped and read it right now. Why, that would be good for you, and I'm not trying to be condescending. I believe that your thoughtful study of this Psalm may lead to an understanding about the concept of righteous power. By the way, my daughter would say that I don't have to *try to be condescending*. She would tell you that it might be a habit of mine, and she would also be kidding. Just as a point of understanding, I consider my comments often to be humorous. As a young child, my sense of humor was a kind of armor against harsh reality. So, I cultivated it and must now work very hard to temper it with wisdom. That's enough about me.

Psalm 18 illustrates an awesome caricature of our Father God's omnipotence. David both understood and respected (yes, feared) God's ultimate power. But at the same time, I think this psalm is David simply saying, "My dad can beat up your dad!" I wish for you to read this testimony of a wounded, sinful, and terrified man and put yourself in his place. You see, David felt that he just never could get it right. What was wrong with him that he could not be faithful and strong and good? Does that sound familiar? Take comfort, dear sister, in these words penned (or warbled) by David. If you feel his pain, then take to heart his knowledge and its accompanying peace. David calls Father his rock, his fortress, his deliverer, strength, shield, and stronghold. He says, "I will call upon the Lord, *who is worthy* to be praised; So shall I be *saved* from my enemies." He spills from his heart all of his deepest fears of death, floods of ungodliness (what a great picture), sorrows of hell, snares and distresses. And, he laments: "I cried out to my God; He heard my voice from His temple, And my cry came before Him, *even* to His ears." David knew that his Heavenly Dad stopped all that He was doing to care for this special son, a man after His own heart. Oh, how He loved David! Sister, He loves you not a tittle less.

The psalm goes on to chronicle God's response to David's plea. David uses words like the earth shook and trembled, the foundations of the hills quaked, smoke went from His nostrils, the fire from His mouth kindled coals. He goes on in his explanation using illustrations like; He flew, He commanded the darkness, clouds and waters, He thundered, with a voice like hailstones of fire, and piercing arrows, He vanquished David's foes with lightening. And then, just like every super hero imaginable, God drew David from the depths of despair and certain destruction, scooped down and delivered him with mercy, lighted his way making his puny way perfect. David needed a savior. So do you and me. Father God sent one for you. *For you.* David concludes:

> The Lord lives!
> Blessed be my Rock!
> Let the God of *my salvation* be exalted—
> And, I sing praises to your name. (Psalm 18:46&49b, emphasis mine)

God Is Our Champion

Can you echo those sentiments? I know that I can. If you want to feel even more special and protected, read on in the 19th psalm: "The law of the Lord is *perfect,* the testimony of the Lord is *sure,* the statutes of the Lord are *right,* the commandment of the Lord is *pure,* the fear of the Lord is *clean,* and the judgments of the Lord are *true and righteous altogether.* More to be desired are they than gold." (Psalm 19:7-10) Whew! Your dad *can* beat up every one else's dad! And, He chose *you* to champion. *You* are His cherished one. *You* are a daughter after His own heart. *You* can count on Him.

God as the Source of All Power

Remember, I told you that your inheritance from Father was to be molded in the image of His Son? We are joint-heirs with Christ. And so, you indeed share in His power. He will strengthen you as He did David. He will lift you up. He will protect you. He will destroy your enemies. You need only to trust in His promises. Trust in His omnipotence. Trust in His love for you. Nothing will bring more peace, joy, and comfort. You can thank Him by using your power for good, asking for His participation in your life and ministry, and *telling Him* as you pray. Go ahead. I'll wait.

I hope that you are at least beginning to feel special and empowered. You cannot share the good news of God's grace and mercy until you are emboldened in these truths. My prayer is that you will continue in your study into this God-given gift of power. In the meantime, let us look at a favorite aspect of Father's character. We *love* this one. So, let's have a little fun with it.

God's Understanding and Sensitive Heart

My husband (God love him) is a hopeless tease. It's okay for me to tell you this. He knows it. He even strives to perfect it. When he cannot tease me, he teases the dog. I don't want you to think that this is the cruel type of teasing. It isn't. It is the I-want-you-to-pay-attention-to-only-me type of teasing, and the I-know-I-can-make-you-laugh-at-yourself type of teasing. Most often, I enjoy this entertainment. If I am busy with other things, I tolerate it. I can't help it. I love him. Anyway, outsiders may consider him to be insensitive. Here is the final truth. He is a big marshmallow with a heart of whipped cream and a spirit easily bruised by injustice. Don't tell his martial arts buddies this. They would never let him hear the end of it! Most of them do not read, so this is just between you and me. (I'm kidding)

Do you recall the story I told you about our little goddaughter? I told you how much I valued and missed her. I told you that I loved her as though she were my own. I haven't told you about the God-ordained relationship my sweet husband had with her.

You know, he wasn't at all experienced in parenting when she came to us. In fact, he was an only child and so did not even have sibling experience. But, from the very second that little baby arrived in our home, he became Father's hands on earth. She was a fitful sleeper, born with the effects of her parent's drug abuse in her little system. Often, she would awaken in the night and want to be with us in bed. Her favorite position was either on top of my face (that's the closest she could get) or feet planted in my husband's side, sprawling out comfortably. I ache with longing for those times. Did my husband grunt and grumble and toss her back into the crib? Not on your life. He would stroke her forehead, brush her hair from her eyes, kiss her cheek, and go and sleep on the couch! When he held her, it was with the tenderness of a saint. He lit up when she came in the room and was saddened when she was not there. Today, he mourns our loss of fellowship, it seems sometimes, more than I. To make matters much worse, we have never been able to have our own children. He is a great source of comfort and support for my grown daughter and loves her with intensity. But, this little child who came and went in the twinkling of an eye, proved him to be a sensitive and awesome father. Today, he shares his concern and affection with the children at our Christian school, praying with them, loving them, and giving them his whole heart. Many have come to the Lord or known true love and commitment from my wonderful husband. How blessed I am! Thank-you, Jesus.

Just in case that is not enough proof for you, my husband is not above shedding genuine tears in the face of the suffering of others, the testimony of others, the gratitude for his blessings, or even a sappy movie. Are you just sick with jealousy? Don't be. I need to remind you that he is a terrible tease. Nobody's perfect.

God Knows Your Pain

Oh excuse me. Someone is perfect. Our Abba Father is perfect. And, as the perfect Father, He is uniquely sensitive to our suffering, pain, and sorrow. We need not look any further than the account of our Savior's last hours on this earth. The ultimate sacrifice was shared by the three persons represented in the Trinitarian God of the Bible. I cannot imagine this intense suffering. Share with me some of those final moments.

One of the dictionary definitions for sensitivity is to be "endowed with sensation". I like that word endowed because it denotes a giftedness that emanates from a magnanimous source—a philanthropist, I suppose. We all love to receive thoughtful gifts and most of us love to give them.

I also like the word sensation. That word brings to mind taste, sight, touch, hearing, and smell. These are our tools for experiencing this planet and its circumstances. As I get older, mine are less "sensitive" and so I appreciate them (and worry about them) more.

Anyway, most of us appreciate it when someone is in tune with what we are feeling or experiencing, especially when it moves him or her to a compassionate act. And, I know that, being a Believer, you consider Christ to be the apex of sensitivity. He is. If you do not relate to the plight of King David, I know you will to another of my most favorite characters in the Bible. Remember, I know you because I share common heartstrings.

God's Love and the Broken Heart

Consider the life of the woman who sought Jesus to worship at his feet with tears and precious oil. If you don't know immediately who that is, you probably are reading this book in order to help someone else. But, I am quite sure that the story of this humble woman strikes a chord in your life. I will confess that this account never fails to bring me to copious tears and trembling. When I get to heaven, I will be visiting her first. What a blessed day that will be!

An Unworthy Woman

This faithful woman was the worst of the worst, the sinner of all sinners, the dregs of society. She sold her body and her self-worth many times. I am certain that she expected to be treated with umbrage and vicious intent. She was. Do you know what else this suffering sinner must have been? She must have been in tune. I believe that God gifted her with that sense of discernment. That convinces me that even when she was immersed in egregious sin, she knew great sorrow and shame. And, through the grace of our Father in Heaven, she knew Jesus when she saw Him. She knew He spoke God's truth because He is God. She knew she needed His forgiveness, and she gave Him her heart. Do you know how I know this? Well, from the Biblical accounts, we know she had a valuable alabaster box filled with precious, fragrant oil. We know enough about the culture of Jesus' time from historians and extra-Biblical sources to understand the significance of this possession. Further, the Bible is clear about the scarcity of these items, the desirability of them, and the meaning of giving them as a gift. These things were prized. So, knowing who Jesus was and understanding her utter need for His blessing, she came into the presence of the Lord bearing gifts and desiring with her whole heart, no matter the consequences, to worship Him. I am in awe.

She was not initially received well. I'm sure you have had moments when you entered a room without a standing ovation. I've even entered a few rooms where the animosity toward me was palpable. I imagine that each step for this wounded and shamed woman was deliberate (so she would not turn and run) and frightening. In her hands, she cradled the priceless balm. The seventh chapter of Luke tells us that she was already weeping.

The room was a buzz with Pharisee disdain. These miscreant religious leaders questioned Jesus' prophetic abilities. Surely, He must know that this woman is not worthy of an audience! If not, He must be a fraud. They were wrong on both counts, as usual, because what happened next is a testimony to all. Frightened and unsure, this sweet pilgrim knelt at the feet of her Savior, her tears, I imagine, cascading onto his holy feet. I know you can understand this. In the life of a wounded child, a literal flood of tears is a common happening. I can almost feel the tightening of the throat, the swelling of the sinuses, and the palpable pain in the chest. My sister, we can relate. So, this pained soul swept up her crowning glory, her hair, and anointed and washed the feet of Jesus with those tears. I remember this scene whenever I am filled with this kind of earthly sorrow. It comes to me often when I meditate on the final hours of our Lord. I am unable to assimilate why Father loved me so much. I cannot imagine what Jesus sees in me. I do not possess gifts fine enough to say thank-you. Like that worshiper at His feet, I can only give Christ what I have. How pitiful am I.

You know that the story does not end there. Humbly, she takes her precious flask and pours the contents onto Jesus' feet. And then, at the advent of this touching worship, the crowd turns nasty, again. The Pharisee (that prince) shares his revulsion that such a one has touched the Lord, filthy sinner that she is. Did Jesus pull away? Did Jesus run from the room? Did Jesus push this broken sister from her place of worship? Nope. Instead, Jesus shared a story with this fine fellow wherein He compared her gifts and praise with the Pharisee's lack thereof. As Jesus often did, He asked a rhetorical question related to debtors and the importance of forgiveness. The more debt we owe, says the Lord, the more love we feel for our Savior. You see, *many* sins are forgiven those who love much. But to those who love little, *little* is forgiven. Which one are you, right now?

Perfect Love

If you are working on being like Jesus, have you forgiven those who trespass against you today? We may be able to put this in the best perspective by returning again to the final hours of our Savior's life.

The air must have been thick with sorrow, even fear. Do you recall that the disciples were pleading for Jesus to stay with them and not to speak of leaving? Remember the vows of loyalty and un-wavering love? Are you disappointed with Peter whose promise did not last the night? I would be if I were not just as guilty of faithlessness in my own life. My students at school are often forced to listen to my accounts of what I call my "Israelite" moments, when I fall into the sin of a lack of trust in my God. I cannot imagine with any real sense the anguish of helplessness felt that night. When I realize that my sinful life was the cause of His suffering, I am shamed and humbled. But, I want us to key on something more than the events. We are talking about sensitivity and compassion here. We wanted that from our dads and did not experience it. It is my hope that you may experience these freely flowing gifts from our Heavenly Father and Jesus. And so, to that end, reflect on those moments sometimes passed over in the passion sequence. In the Garden of Gethsemane after the Sufferer's blood flowed from His pores, the Lord found the strength of character to heal the severed ear of one of his accusers. On the cross, in abject and unparalleled pain, Jesus forgave his tormentors and intervened with Father for them. Christ in this most unbearable time remembered to secure a surrogate son for his mother in the person of John the Beloved. Hanging in torment, the Savior of the world assured the humbled thief that he would be with Him in paradise and gave peace to a fearful and sinful heart. My point? I can't even speak with gentleness to my child when I have a headache! Do you think that Jesus will turn *you* away or does not know what you are going through? He knows. He feels your pain. He understands your suffering, and He reaches out to you even now. Take His hand. Bask in His loving and gentle concern. Drink it in and go in peace. And hear His Holy Word:

> Remember my affliction and roaming,
> The wormwood and the gall,
> My soul still remembers
> And sinks within me.
> This I recall to my mind,
> Therefore I have hope,
> Through the Lord's mercies, we are not consumed,
> Because His compassions fail not.
> They are new every morning;
> Great is your faithfulness.
> The Lord is my portion says my soul,
> Therefore I hope in Him. (Lamentations 3:22-24)

The Bible Is a Love Letter

Now then, I know what you are thinking. You know that Jesus is God and you are not. He can do all things and you cannot. God is perfect, and I'm laughing at the next phrase. (You know: He is, you aren't.) The laughter is medicinal, but the point is still taken. We can never be God. He is transcendent. He is totally other. Then, how can we relate to Him or feel His relationship to us? The simple answer is that He told us how He feels. And, the beauty of this is that when God says something, His behavior is consistent with His Word. This is foreign to little sisters who are told one thing and see another, right? Our Father God seems to have felt that He could not tell us that He loves us enough. It is all over The Book. He wants you to know that He has great compassion on you. Forever and ever His love is with you. He desires you to come and live in His shelter. He will rescue you from every trap *and* the fatal plague, shield you with His wings, shelter you with His feathers, be your armor and protection, and even when a thousand fall at your side, or ten thousand are dying around you, evils will not touch you. He loves you that much and HE KEEPS HIS PROMISES!

Jesus Has Known Your Sorrow

You see, Father wants to have fellowship with you so much that He sent His Son into this world to take on a mortal body for His glory and your salvation. All of these messages are written in His Holy Word. Still you ask, does God really understand me and my situation? You are a tough one, so let me give you a visual.

Imagine the last time you saw a goofy movie with a genie in a bottle. Now, I'm certainly not comparing our Lord with anything so base. But as a little child, did you ever wonder with awe about how that big, old, powerful, genie could scrunch himself into a tiny bottle? You and I cannot even grasp the unfathomable concept of God reducing Himself to human form. When He did this, all of the physical paraphernalia that comes with flesh was experienced in that body. Jesus felt physical pain. Jesus felt earthly groanings. Jesus probably skinned His knee as a child, hammered His finger, had a headache, or bumped His funny bone. You do not have to continue to believe in a god who does not feel your pain. He did and He does. So, is God sensitive to our plight and our needs? I would say that He is uniquely sensitive. He created the lump of clay that is you. He lowered himself into one for you. And, He knows how you feel.

God Gives Us Boldness

Now, I know that your dad might not have understood you. In fact, he may not have considered understanding you to be on his top ten to-do list. There is little time in this life to be disappointed by a lack of character in another. Sin will never go out of style and, in the case of your fellowship with your dad, you must leave the area until he gets well. The path homeward is rocky, often steep, and treacherous. Father waits for you there. If you believe in the great love He has for you, your duty is to fight the good fight and do unto others. While you are formulating your game plan, we will move on to another family trait handed down to God's kids – boldness. Keep your hands and feet inside the car for this one.

God as Our Companion

I can think of nothing more pleasant to do with a lazy weekend than to spend it with good friends and family. At the end of a disheartening and dizzying week, I want comfort and cheer. I want to laugh, cry, sing out loud, and dance. I want to settle back into a mountain of pillows and sigh, A LOT. This may not be your perfect weekend. If you are one of those gymnasium or water sports kind of gals, you go sister! My point is that it is sheer joy to fill your life with genuine people who care about you and desire your company. Who else will listen to your theory about where missing sox go in the laundry? Only your closest confidants will sit still long enough for you to wax philosophical.

And so, when we are in need of regeneration and recharging, we choose good, old, down-home company. Our Father in Heaven is that kind of good, down-home company. But, you may ask, how can I, in my guilty state, presume to ask the Creator God to cradle my beaten body at the end of a long journey? We wonder what we have to offer our Father that He might value. As a small, insignificant child, I think you wondered that about your earthly father. Many of us internalized an absence of self-value in the presence of our dad.

Perhaps your experience was minimal, settling around a general overall sense of missing the mark or coming in second. Dads often are hamstrung with functional disabilities and may totally neglect a little daughter's need for encouragement. Dads sometimes fly by a little girl hoping to "find time" another day. Dads even strike an emotional or physical blow as they rush to a more important event. If you were in the path of an apathy typhoon or a criticizing hurricane, I love you. You are my sister. Be at peace. Jesus came to lift you up. God seeks you for companionship. The Bible contains the invitation to all Believers to come "boldly" into His throne room, no hanging of the head or twiddling of the fingers, but a head up, eye-to-eye, heart-to-heart entrance. The Lord is saving you a big, fluffy pillow at His feet where He can reach to stroke your hair. It reminds me of the golden times I would gather at my mother's feet as she cooked or ironed (that's where a large, hot, metal implement forces the wrinkles out of your clothing-- just kidding!). The moments of peace and contentment under mom's care are priceless memories now that she is gone. But the feeling is the same. My Father God waits for you and me. Fly to Him in prayer and supplication. Spend your devotionals in His presence. Read to Him. Read about Him. Worship His Name. Go boldly. Wait. I said go *boldly*. He will always be there and you can always gain audience. Our God does not have to find time for you. He *made* time. He can make more.

When God Says It, That's Final

I would be remiss in my duty if I did not remind you at this point in our discussion that God *will* always have the last word. As you gain confidence in His presence, remember that you are an instrument in His hands created *for* good works. The scripture will point you toward your ministry and as you learn and grow in The Lord, He will set you on the right path. But, you must be with Him often. Read and pray. Read and pray. Worship and adore. Sing and praise. Answers will come and your spot in the throne room will become familiar. You will not lose your seat. Finally, go and invite someone else's pinched face inside. We're drowning out here!

Spread God's Peace

Before we leave this important subject, let me make one final point. The adults in the household set the tone of the household. Now, a gentle and nurturing mother is vital to a peace-filled home. We all know the old saying: "If mom ain't happy, ain't nobody happy!" I'm sure you can accept your responsibility in this project. When you leave God's throne room, bring His peace and love into your front room. Then stand back and watch the Lord work in the lives of your family. I know that this may be a tall order because in many homes the phrase, "Wait until your father gets home" means there will soon be a change in tone.

Maybe your father brought fear, anguish, and dread home from work. As a child, you were powerless to mount an offensive against sin of this magnitude. Some of you may have permanent finger depressions inside your ears from trying to block out the scary sounds.

Today is a new day. You are a big girl and you can change the cycle. Stay focused on Christ, continue your daily devotionals, pray for strength and peace, and get help with the determination of a puppy trying to get peanut butter off of his top lip. (Mind you. I do not recommend this type of entertainment.) Remember, all things work together for good for those who are in Christ Jesus. Your Father will discipline your dad. Your husband will be brought into line. Your Dad is bigger than his.

What about Perfect Justice?

Well, this has been a wonderful journey so far. I say this because I might be about to lose some of you, and I would feel badly if I did not tell you what a great time I have had. I'm getting to know you and I like that. I will miss you if you leave now. I just cannot put off the next discussion, as I now begin to explore God's justice. This is not usually our favorite character trait. I hope to change your mind. But, if you can't stand the heat—No. Wait a minute. You stay right where you are! We are in for the long haul, right? I promised you peace at the *end* of my story. You can't bail now. Grab a woobie (comfort blanket) and keep readin'. It will be worth it.

We all know God is perfect. He is the perfect Father. He is a perfect gentleman. He is perfect in every way. Unfortunately, He is the deliverer of perfect justice. Nothing that is not perfectly just can exist in God's presence. Relax. We know that our Father in Heaven sees us through the shed blood of Jesus. Whew! The throne room door is still open. However, God is perfectly just and must punish sin and disobedience. He disciplines those He loves. You are His loved one and, therefore, will be taken to the woodshed as often as needed. Now, I don't know about you, but I am a slow learner. I seem to be in the woodshed a lot. In fact, some days I am just dense and can't see the forest for the woodshed! (I am so hoping that you get that.) I'll share an illustration so that you will.

Our Own Imperfection

I am a teacher in our Christian School. It is a small school, and so I am also the Administrator. That means that when a child must go to the principal's office, he finds himself in front of my desk. Now then, I don't believe myself to be particularly scary or intimidating. However, when a child messes up badly enough to "need to speak to Joyce", he or she does so with great fear. I am convinced that they are afraid because, in the usual course of the day, we are all great friends and they love me. Next train to fantasyland leaving at gate six! No, really. I have proof in the form of love letters and notes of gratitude. When they must come for discipline, they often feel ashamed and sorry to have disappointed me. It works like a charm. Anyway, there are certain rules and ideals that are inviolate in our school. The students know what they are and I know how to use them. I tell you this story to get to the real illustration.

Even on my worst day with a headache and bad attitude, I will never get the award at the year-end for the most stringent discipline. That dubious honor must be given to the students themselves. You see, most teachers try lots of techniques throughout their careers to stabilize their classrooms. They will often try the what-do-you-think-should be-your-punishment trick. I can testify to you that neither courtroom, nor judge could possibly come up with the nasty consequences recommended by a class of third graders. They consider an entire school year without lunch to be just punishment for pushing in line. In their tiny minds, suspension is the perfect solution to gum chewing. They will even suggest that they receive a paddling every day for a year for not returning a book. Talk about a tough room! I know that a reasonable adult would temper this type of torture with a more fitting condition. But you see, even these youngsters understand that rules are in place to keep them safe and in control and healthy. Kids don't like a free-for-all attitude. It scares them. We are, however, like cattle in that our first activity when turned loose in the corral is to walk around the fence and test our boundaries. That's our sin-nature creeping out. Father said there is none, not one, who does not fall short of the glory of God. I will confess guilty to that charge.

By The Refining Fire

But by nature of contrast, think back on a time you observed some high drama in a real courtroom. It is becoming more and more common for the bad guy to walk free and his crimes to be marginalized. The Biblical charge of the government to protect the righteous and punish the guilty is fading fast as our country turns its face from our first love.

God is perfectly just. He must punish sin. He cannot co-exist with unrighteousness. That would violate His promise to be consistent and holy. He will never do that. His commandments are in place to bring us safety, peace, and joy. His perfect justice is our shelter. I know it does not always feel like that when you are in the throes of discipline, but the refiner's fire will bring you forth as gold. Ouch and amen.

And so, we must strive to be just in all we do. King David, just before his death, advised his son Solomon:

> . . . keep the charge of the Lord your God, to walk in His ways, to keep His statutes, His commandments, His judgments, and His testimonies, as it is written in the Law of Moses, that you may prosper in all that you do and wherever you turn. (1 Kings 2:3)

The Importance of the Law

I think the law and the rules were pretty important, don't you? Solomon went on to become the King famous for solving the dilemma between two women who wanted the same baby. In the light of justice, the real mother proved herself worthy of the name and the false mother was exposed as a wicked liar. His father, David, gave him good advice and he followed suit. Justice is not a dirty word. It is manna from heaven in a dying and dreary world. I would guess that whatever your father did to harm you would be best served if it were appropriately punished. You would be vindicated and he would have another chance perhaps to be forgiven and restored. If you are not ready for that, it's okay.

Solomon had prayed for God's wisdom and he received it. He did not always perform so admirably. But, our Father in Heaven does. Justice is your friend. Jesus is your best friend. Give thanks for it learn to apply it in your own life. David said it best in Psalm 119 as he vowed to delight in the law of the Lord and to meditate on it day and night. Moses sang of it in Deuteronomy 32:4:

> He is the Rock. His work is perfect;
> For all His ways are justice, a God
> Of truth and without injustice;
> Righteous and upright is He.

We are created in God's image. We can delight in the Law, study it, and practice it in our lives. It's in The Book. You no longer need wander in the wilderness. The answers to your questions and needs are on its pages. How good God is!

Well, are you still there? If you are, you made it. Give yourself a big pat on the shoulders and sit back and enjoy the next message. I saved the best for last. We are embarking on tender territory again so keep the tissue box close by, and remember that once we are in the air, you may not leave the plane. (I always wanted to say that.)

Abba Father's Plan for You

There are few sounds more beautiful in this world than the gurgle of an infant, happily enfolded in peaceful play. It is musical and magical. I could listen all day. What parent is not ecstatic when that tiny gurgle turns into those sacred words, mommy and daddy. You heard me right. I said sacred. Parenthood is God-ordained. It is the stuff for which we are created. It is most certainly not *the only* reason, but it's big. Those who study the Bible in depth know of a special Aramaic word, Abba. It is the single most breathtaking title I know. Simply put, it means daddy. And, it refers to our Father in Heaven. In fact, it is the term used by Jesus in addressing His Father. That there is a special Aramaic word for daddy is not surprising. But, that it refers to a special bond God has with you is awesome.

I do not wish to burst your bubble if you do not know this, but you are adopted. Now, that's a little joke to introduce to you the concept of Abba Father.

This is the Father who knew you before you were born. This is the Father who gave His Son to assure your home with Him. And, this is the Father who came looking for you when you were lost. This shepherd, this King, this daddy, came after you with jealousy and righteous intent. He was not content that you be lost any more. If you are still waiting to be swooped up into loving arms, reach up! The fact that you are continuing to read this book indicates to me that you are, likely, His child. You desire fellowship with Him. He has located you on His radar and is reeling you in, as we speak. Daddy has come to get His little girl. Thank-you is such a small word.

Still not convinced? Do not tempt me! By now you know I can get tough. Therefore, I can share this with you now.

A Loving Parent

As a young mother, I was bowled over by the love I felt for my sweet daughter. There was not a moment in the day or night that I did not want to be with her. She was beauty, perfection, grace, and love all rolled into one receiving blanket. I could not believe that I had carried her in my body or that I had ever deserved this blessed gift. As I recall it today, she is 35 years old and I am still humbled by my love for her and God's love for me. After she was born, I wanted dozens of them. This was the most remarkable thing I had ever known. For many long years, I waited for another gift from The Lord. It never came. I reveled in the relationship I had with my baby girl. I will be forever grateful for her life. But, I longed for more children. I *ached* for more children. The choking tears were never far from the surface. The regular disappointment became almost a life sentence. That I would never give birth to another child became the greatest sorrow of my life. And, when late in my life, Abba Father blessed me with a wonderful and godly husband, (after an abusive first marriage) the pain of infertility inflamed and became an ever-blackening source of grief. My husband, a true lover of God, suffers great sorrow over not having a child. From time to time, I see him struggle with this deep sadness and continue to respond with a faith just as deep in His Father, who is sovereign over all. How I love him!

Several times, we have attempted to adopt a child, each time to have our dreams and hopes dashed. We bundle the baby clothes and the bottles and diapers away to a dark corner and go on with our lives and ministry. Maybe, you have been there too. If you have, then listen carefully. Your desire for a child does not even compare to the desire of our Abba Father to have you home with him for eternity. You were lost. He came looking for you. He *will not* let you go. Nothing can take you from Him. This daddy values you far above rubies, gold, or silver. Abba will not fail.

My sister, live your life in this knowledge. Fatherhood is sacred. You are precious. Your mortal father was or is not equal to this task. Let it go. Pray for him. Turn to your true Father and He will lift you up. It is your sacred promise.

Chapter Two

What Is a Daughter?

Rejoice greatly, O daughter of Zion!
Shout, O daughter of Jerusalem!
Behold, your King is coming to you; . . .
—Zech. 9:9a

WHEN I was a young mother, my mother, my sisters, and I would gather occasionally for what we called ladies day. Simply put, there we no kids allowed. Usually, we were celebrating one another's birthdays, but sometimes we just went out for a Saturday lunch. Did I remember to say that there were no kids allowed? That part was special because all of my sisters, along with my mother, were awesome moms. I'm talking about moms who cooked, sewed, built tent houses, made gallons of punch drinks for every kid in the neighborhood, and served as PTA president. From the top down, our family made a solemn commitment to motherhood. And so, when we were out without the kids, it was a time for celebration. Often, that meant real-live grown-up talk, punctuated by precious moments of complete silence. These were glorious times. However, due to our nerves, we could never manage to extend these times much past an hour and a half. That was our best shot—1 1/2 hours. After that, each of us began to get anxious in the realization that we did not know what the kids were up to. As a funny side note, my sisters and I still get together today for ladies day. Our children are all grown and we still cannot maintain the party attitude for longer than an hour and a half. (Old dogs—old tricks) Still, I do not want you to miss the most important detail of these sister days. My mother was there with us. My mother was out with her daughters for special time alone together in sweet fellowship. This memory endures as one of my most prized.

Defining Moments

So, just what does it mean to be someone's daughter? More pointedly, what does it mean to be your father's daughter? Step aside. The floodgates are now opening wide. If you have not already done so, get your woobie or a big, fluffy pillow to hold to your stomach. It's okay right now. Just don't take it to church or a job interview. That's a red flag. Now take a deep breath. Cleanse. Cleanse.

The dictionary defines a daughter as a female child or person in relation to her parents. By now you know that I am not comfortable with such clinical definitions. I am aware that, at its foundation, this is an acceptable condensation of the concept. I also know that, included in that concept, are many complexities that tell us about the personhood and value of a daughter. Just to introduce our topic, allow me to share one of my greatest failures with you.

I cannot grow a plant. There. I said it. Please don't think that if you just teach me or I just pay attention, you are sure I could grow a plant. Step away from the chalkboard! Many have tried before you and I do not have the heart to disappoint another sweet spirit. All kidding aside, the proverbial green thumb is a gift. Some's got it. Some don't. I don't. I do, however, have a life's technique for dealing with this failure. I always purchase plants that are very common and easily found. Then you see, I buy small ones and when they croak, I just go back to the nursery and buy another one just like it, a tiny bit bigger. That way, people think I'm doing just fine. Don't act so surprised, because I have warned you about me. I also thank you for bearing with me as I make this point.

Every plant has certain needs that are common to all chlorophyll-producing organisms. They require food, light, and carbon dioxide. There are other substances needed in a more complex scheme, but the basic three will suit our story. Suffice to say that without the basic three, the plant will be "no more". We must also understand that different kinds of plants may need different kinds of substances to support healthy life—more water, less water, more food, less food, and so on.

How Does Your Daughter Grow?

That is how it is with daughters. Praise God alone that I have been a much better mother than plant lady. Still, the comparison works. It is just good thinking to know that various little girls needs may be different because of their unique character or circumstances. However, *all* daughters need those foundational substances to grow. We all need food, water, shelter, oxygen, and love. Yep. I said we *need* love, and I mean it. Study after study would support that infants do not thrive without love no matter how adequately the basic life support items are provided. These five things are basic and children must count on their adults to provide them.

That brings us to a female child, organically relating, while desperately trying to emotionally relate to her parents. To be fair, not all little daughters are in desperate circumstances. It is just that, since you are reading this book, it may be that you were or are. I have not forgotten that this part of our conversation is about a daughter's needs. And so, I begin a list that will never be finished because there are so many of you out there, all so much alike and all so unique. You might say that we are all limited editions of the same idea. Nevertheless, it is comforting to know that perhaps all of us can relate in some way to the suggestions on this list.

What a Girl Needs

Okay. I believe that you have a need to be appreciated as a perfect creation. That girl who grimaces at you from your bathroom mirror each day may not seem to be a perfect creation. In fact, you have had a few years to memorize your faults and weaknesses. You have also had more than a few especially challenging days related to your hair, skin, or figure. Each of us has burdens to bear. We usually bear them in our own way, but could agree that we have many similarities with each other. So, aside from breakouts, bad hair days, and the battle of the bulge, what do you see in your mirror? You understand that your mirror is merely a reflective device that has a limited task. It reflects. It is the heart and mind creating the reflection that holds the power over us. We all have an objective reflection modified by a subjective reality. Those are smart-sounding words meaning; we all see what we believe to be true and that vision may not connect with reality. Anorexia and bulimia are epidemic because of this. I think that it is important to stand there by your side for a few moments and talk about what *you* see.

The Wonder of His Love

A little girl's father can be a powerful influence on what she sees in her reflection. I think about all of the sweet children who spend each day under the specter of constant criticism. For whatever reason, their dad feels the need to correct, correct, correct. I could wax philosophical about why fathers take this role, but that is not what we are sharing about right now. A daughter who can never seem to do anything right or well enough will become discouraged and depressed often accepting the belief that she is inferior. Her need to feel appreciated is invalidated and relegated to a dark lockbox marked: *Do Not Open—Ever!* And so, she never sees an accurate reflection. She sees herself through a distorted lens all clouded up with her dad's dysfunctional view. Some of you know what this feels like. Some of you are tough, really tough and you survived this toxic environment by forming a resolve to "prove the old guy wrong". That was good. You are strong. But, most of you are still not seeing through the glass, clearly. It still hurts when you hear the word stupid or ugly or awkward, ad infinitum.

A prominent learning theory would support that if you tell a child something 25 times, he or she will believe it. It tears at my heart that some of you heard the same criticism 25 times a day or an hour or a minute. And so, today you face your bathroom mirror and tell it to yourself. You know how destructive that is and so, I'm going to help you change it. Do not look into that mirror another time until you internalize this next concept. Our Heavenly Father created each one of us to be different—one you, one me. No one else has ever been or ever will be like us. If I miss knowing you, I cannot reclaim the experience ever. I will be less of a person for not having known you. This morning, God counted the hairs on your head. He heard the desires of your heart. He blessed your going and your coming. He sent angels to see you safely there. Father God made you in His image and has plans for your future. He gifted you with special talents and abilities for His own glory. When you use those special gifts with integrity, God blesses and appreciates you. Your daily reflection becomes more beautiful as you radiate God's purpose in your life. There is a volume switch on those old messages from your dad. Turn them off. Replace that old song with a new one. Try:

> I will praise You, for I am fearfully and wonderfully made;... (Psalm 139:14a)

Everything about you is full of wonder. Your new bathroom message should be from the Father of all "I breathed life into you and you are wonderful, wonderful, wonderful." If you have to, say it 25 times per day until you believe it. The Lord of all believes it. In fact, Jesus has a stripe with your name on it. Boy, are you something! I thank God for you. Please glorify your Father in your wonderful reflection today.

How God Sees You

Aside from a need to be appreciated, girls need to be noticed. There is a bazillion dollar industry out there aimed at making us beautiful. But, I am not necessarily talking about the way we deck ourselves out to get noticed. Motivation for beauty rituals can be legion. I am asking you to entertain the concept that girls need to be truly *seen* by the people who are important in their lives. I wanted my daddy to notice that I was in the room with him, or that I was wearing a new dress. I wanted him to *see* me. It was seldom the case, unless I had made a bad choice and needed improvement. That makes me think of something. Surprise!

I had the very special experience of playing the lead in the Thornton Wilder play "Our Town". There is a scene where my character, Emily, dies and is allowed to return to her life for one day before beginning her eternal rest. She chooses to re-experience her 12th birthday, to the dismay of the other dearly departed folks, who warn her against choosing any day with special significance. Well, the excitement is just overwhelming as Emily re-lives that birthday. She stands again by her mother in their kitchen as breakfast is being prepared, sees her father running down the stairs to run off to work, and relishes the joy of being with them. And then, she notices something. They are all talking, but no one is *looking*. Frantically, Emily pleads with her family to just *look at her*. The need to really connect that one last time is filled with quiet desperation. When Emily realizes that she cannot change the past and the indifference with which her loved ones revolved around each other, she sadly leaves the scene. But, the real tearjerker is her soliloquy in which she bids a final farewell to new-ironed dresses, rain on the roof, her hometown, and her mama and papa. Not a dry eye in the house.

How painful it is for a little girl to be a non-person in her father's eyes. What a longing there is in that tiny heart to be looked at with love. You know what I mean. You can see it in someone's eyes when they really care about you. Assertive children grab their parent's faces in their hands and force them to look in their eyes. That's how we know we are important. Eye contact means you are really listening. It means you think we are worth the effort. You *see* us. There is not a day that could possibly be so busy that it disallows time to look at your baby. I know how much it hurt to be ignored by your dad. I was ignored unless I needed to be criticized. Now I am a show-off. Go figure.

Our Father in Heaven checks up on us every minute of every day. He does not take breaks or naps. He does not leave the office and turn on the voice mail. He watches you as you lie down and when you rise up. There is no place you can go to hide from Him. Raise a holy hand and wave hello right now. He will see you. It is okay to need to be noticed. You are awesome and should be seen. In fact, part of my frustration in writing this book is that, I cannot see your face. I would love that. I am sure it is worth seeing.

The Hope of Understanding

That brings me to the next need daughters have. We all need to be understood.

In my work with children with disabilities, I often worked with little ones with speech or language delays. It is hard enough to understand the emerging language of an allegedly normal preschooler. When you are trying to understand a child with a communication deficit, it can be a guessing game, at best. What I learned was to listen and respond anyway. We asked questions. We blamed our broken brains or slow ears to avoid blaming the child. The children who felt understood, got better faster. They had much less frustration to compound the problem. The need to be understood is a basic need for all humans. It goes hand-in-hand with the need to know that our ideas and donations are worthy. We have talked at length about our God coming to this earth into a body unworthy of His station. But, His experiences in that body gave Him a total understanding of what it means to be human. And so, He understands your physical and emotional pains. Do you know what else the Bible says? It says that God *knows* your heart. Oh-oh. Dive! Dive! (You know I'm kidding) I just want you to know that Father knows your fears, your desires, your hopes and dreams, and your secrets. No matter what is in there, if you are His child, He loves you. He will not stop loving you. He has claimed you as His. You cannot be left behind.

Writing Your Letter to God

A few years ago as I led a women's conference, I wrote a poem and read it. I wanted to introduce an exercise that I recommend to you now. I asked the ladies to write a letter to God. They were to tell Him everything. Purge, if you will. Picture a room full of women, feverishly writing, pens and paper flying, tears flowing, and sighs ascending. I promised them what I promise you now. Father God will listen, care, and understand. He wants to hear from you. He desires your fellowship. He misses you. Try it. And, just to get you started, here is the poem:

> Tell Him your sorrows.
> Tell Him your pain.
> Tell Him your needs,
> And, tell Him again.

Give Him your heartbreak.
Give Him your tears.
Give Him your sadness
And, give Him your fears.

Tell Him you trust Him.
Tell Him you don't.
Tell Him you need Him.
He can't leave you—He won't.

Now, write your letter. I've got lots of time.

God's Instructional Discipline

A daughter also needs to be taught how to succeed. That means, she needs to be trained and disciplined. Nothing good ever came from in-activity. And, self-esteem is built largely upon the objective proof that we are capable, that we can make things work, that we have power over our choices and our environment, and that we know the rules. A confidant person is safe and joyful. A frightened person is frozen and alone.

There are as many ways to teach these lessons as there are good people with healthy motives to teach them. We know what to teach because we have the definitive curriculum in God's Word. Proverbs is a super place to begin. I happen to prefer the do-as-I-do method or the modeling technique. When your child sees you doing good things, he or she will go and do likewise. Sadly, the opposite is true. If you are a person of low integrity, your kids are watching and learning from you. Usually, wounded little girls do not follow in their father's footsteps if he was the bad role model. They will often take a rubber band jump to the opposite end of the scale, taking great pride in *not* being like their father. Sometimes, this valiant attempt to "right the old wrongs" causes cynical or negative behavior that puts others off and leaves great sadness in its wake. I use the rubber band illustration in the hope that these girls will eventually relax a little and find a comfortable resting place somewhere in between the behaviors they hate and the ones they fake. Still, daughters need to know how to behave and how to become the best child of God that they can. Therefore, our Father in Heaven gave us some commandments, some rules, and some directions.

We have already learned that we are created in God's image and are joint-heirs with Christ. And I think the do-as-I-do model applies here. The Trinitarian God of the Bible models all of the character traits that are to be passed down to us.

He has shown thee, O man, what is good
and what the Lord desires of thee.
But, to live justly, and to love mercy,
and to walk humbly with our God. (Micah 6:8)

You know that is just the beginning. The Bible is full of directions and you can read them and fill your life with joy and a greater sense of purpose. Or, you could stop now, feel over-loaded, and miss something of value. I know you are not a quitter, so I continue.

We All Need Encouragement

All little girls need to feel validated and encouraged by their dads. You notice that I carefully chose the word encouraged here. There is a difficult to discern difference between encouragement and praise. If you learn that difference, it will serve you well as you raise children or associate with God's people. God is encouraging. We praise Him. We are encouraged. He is praised. Hold on. I'm going to explain it. I know what you are thinking. Here comes another story. Look how clever you are!

For this story to work, you must believe that children are easy to manipulate. As parents, we like to call that concept motivation. However you dress it up, we all use techniques to direct a child's path and increase the incidence of a desired behavior or decrease the occurrence of an undesirable one. We have already learned that parents must first outline the fence and establish the rules. That said, a focused parent notices a child's efforts and comments on the outcome. Lots of little girls were damaged by negative comments from their fathers. At the same time, any positive or seemingly approving comments were like manna in the wilderness. You see, what we need is to know that we have done well or that we are on the right track. We will most often repeat a behavior that has brought us pleasure and discard a behavior that has resulted in pain.

So here you are, an adorable and sweet, little princess, waiting for input or at the least a reaction to your antics. I can imagine that you may have grown up on pins and needles or in a room full of eggshells like I did. Step, crunch! Step, ouch! Freeze and retreat. What a daughter needs is to be encouraged in every experience. We needed our daddy to say that we had good ideas, that he loved seeing our pictures, and that he could name the colors that we used. We did not need to be corrected when we colored outside the lines or thought of a way to put up a playhouse that may have looked more like a war zone. Encouraging phrases comment on the processes and progress of learning and sharing and appreciate any and all efforts to move forward in a positive, growing way. How I would have loved to hear my father say: "Thank-you for spending time with me sweetheart." Actually, if he had ever called me sweetheart, I believe it would have lived within me forever. I think you know what I mean. You see, my dad did not need to tell me how my efforts fell short. He needed to encourage me to keep trying until I succeeded. Let me illustrate.

There Is More Than One Way to Cut the Pie

We have a little family joke that is one of those bittersweet ones. I can laugh at it, but it still strikes a sour chord. You need some background in order to "get" this joke. Thanksgiving is a big time for my family. We gather in large numbers around several long tables to eat, talk, and interrupt each other. Now my mother was an amazing and prolific cook, so we never lacked for food at a family celebration. Dad often teased her about her quantity cooking with comments like: "*You had better bring in the third turkey, Lois. The kids are looking faint,*" or "*Do you think there are enough homeless folks in town to eat the leftovers, or should we call the papers?*" I don't think he was mean-spirited. I think it was teasing that had lost its power years before. Mom did not care about his attitude. She did not want to run out of food. As an aside, our family was huge. There were seven children and each of us dragged home a wife or husband and children by the car-full. And, that brings me to my story.

At one Thanksgiving, I was positioned at the end of the pie table. Yes, you heard me right. We had an entire table full of pies. Lest you do not appreciate what I just shared, it was not a card table. So, there I was sitting by the pie-o-rama. One of my little nieces desired a piece of pumpkin pie and stood by me in an attempt to cut a piece. Now then, I love children. Did I tell you that? And so, I steadied the pie pan and watched her position and re-position the knife, pushing and sawing to release the treat to her dish. It was very close to mush. All of this occurred in seconds and all the while that I was enjoying and supporting this learning experience, my sisters and my mother were cringing in agony. Finally, one sister could no longer contain her anguish. "You are cutting the pie all wrong, *honey.*" (That word *honey* can sound like a swear sometimes.) Oh, my, cutting the pie all wrong. Alert the media! Thanksgiving has been ruined! I can now see the silliness of this situation. But, that day among the nodding heads of sisters and mother, that little one stopped trying and waited to be served. I am not the most popular member of my family with the adults. I responded by encouraging my niece to continue, applauded her effort, and smiled, yes, right into her eyes as she walked away with a plate full of glops, proud and happy. I got the glares. She got the pie.

You Are God's Workmanship and His Word Will Guide You

Because you have similar stories, I know you get it. Of course, some things must be done the right way. No one wants you to wire your house without the instructions and the expertise. But please, many things can be accomplished hundreds of ways without the earth tilting on its axis. The discoveries through the ages that have impacted us the most were uncovered, largely, by coincidence or accident. A little daughter must be encouraged to step out and try. If your father slapped you down when you did that, make a new resolve. He is not controlling your every move anymore. (At least, not physically.) Try again. There is no right way to cut the pie. Relax. And, turn to the people in your care and in your circle of influence and smile right in their eyes in approval. What can it hurt you? Your gifts are not gifts if they are kept hidden. Do not hide your light under a bushel. Let it shine!

By the way, the inherent problem with praising a child is the danger that you may set them up to require approval in all things. Today, daddy likes your picture. But, maybe tomorrow, he will not. One day, you are pretty. But the next day, you may not make the grade. When your self-esteem is completely tied up in the approval of others, you are at the whims of public opinion. Surely, you could be thinner, smarter, richer, better. This is the stuff that keeps us all screaming for help wherever a therapy shingle swings. I won't be-labor this point. I would invite you to study it more. Hey. I know. What does our Father in Heaven suggest?

Well, Abba Father has chosen you as His special child and servant. He has called you to be His hands and feet. He has promised never to leave or reject you. He has even promised to strengthen you and hold you up as you step out in faith. He will hold the plate while you cut the pie. That alone should be enough. Only, it was not enough for your Father who loves you. He went right ahead and sent a Helper.

> And, I will pray the Father, and He will give you another Helper, that He may abide with you forever---the Spirit of truth, whom the world cannot receive, because it neither sees Him nor knows Him; but you know Him, for

> He dwells with you and will be in you.
> I will not leave you orphans; I will
> come to you. (John 14:16-18)

This Helper comforts, strengthens, and gives you power. You can have face-to-face fellowship with this Comforter whenever you are on your knees. Most of all, I want you, dear sister, to anticipate the message Father will have for you when you stand in eternity. And, like the faithful servant in the account in Matthew 25, verse 21, you may hear: *"Well done, good and faithful servant. You were faithful over a few things. I will make you ruler over many things. Enter into the joy of your lord."* That is encouragement at its finest.

How God Uses His Daughters

This means you have work to do. There is a ministry with your name on it. Go and encourage someone, today. And, stand back because God will bless your efforts like you cannot imagine. You are set apart for His work because you are the perfect one to do it. He has prepared you for great things. I encourage you to trust in the Lord with all your heart and lean not on your own understanding. And especially, do not put stock in the sinful ramblings of others as they try to discourage your walk. They are not aware of with whom they are dealing. (I teach English, also.)

If you have taken the last message into your heart, this next lesson will go quickly. Young daughters need to feel useful and needed. We want to make a contribution. We hope to see things change due to our efforts. Maybe your father kept you stuck and thinking that you did not have anything to offer. You gave up early on believing that your contribution was somehow unworthy. After all, who would want your help, advice, or opinion? My dad said my ideas were stupid. I responded by deifying intellect. This led me into a complete meltdown in my forties. By the way, all the time I was convincing myself that I was the smartest person in the room, I was making some of the worst decisions since the decision to leave some of the lifeboats off of *The Titanic*.

I just wanted to give you permission to make the best casserole at the potluck and feel a sense of accomplishment when people enjoy it. I want you to go ahead and feel a little smug when you bring sweaters to the picnic because you know it will be cold later in the day, and bask in the appreciation of your chilly children. Feel free to put real velour pinafores on the church flannel board figures and accept compliments at their beauty. Take some canned goods to the church storehouse. Give your neighbors a loaf of bread. Volunteer at the Christian School. (Please!) Make your mark and feel good about it. You are needed. You are valuable. You are God's, little girl created *for* good works. It will make your day. I promise.

What's Love Got to Do with It?

Of course, the most precious need a daughter has is the need to be loved. I know that many of the aforementioned concepts would fit neatly in this box. Still, I think this subject needs its own treatise. What does it mean to be loved? What would feel like love to you? How badly do we need it and where do we need it to originate? Let's get going. This will take a while.

I began this section by including love as a primary-level need. I equate this requirement with food, water, and air. Many folks, more educated than I, have come to this conclusion. But, if you remember back to beginning of the book, I admitted that I am not a psychologist. I am like you and have struggled through a life filled with learning experiences and a few great opportunities for formal educational pursuits. We could go on to explore the myriads of studies that speak to this subject or we could stroke the floor with our fuzzy slippers and chat among ourselves. I like the last idea best.

Love, a Non-Example

To start us off, I want you to meet Sarah (not her real name). Sarah was a preschool student of mine years ago. She was a bit of a puzzle. Most of her developmental skills were appropriate for her age. She was four. She could hop, slide, run, and jump. She could color, finger paint, and string beads. She put pegs in a pegboard just fine. She recognized her name. She sang the alphabet song and knew every verse to the Bus Song.

The puzzle was that whenever I asked her to draw a picture of herself, the product was disappointing. Sarah could barely draw an awkward circle for a head, but the rest of the drawing was not discernable. Other body parts were indiscriminately strewn around the paper. Her facial features were not drawn. Sometimes, Sarah would place two dots, without formulation, somewhere inside the lopsided, circle head. She was just trying to please me and make an attempt at drawing her eyes. I was encouraging, but I was also puzzled and concerned. What could possibly keep this adorable child from producing some kind of self-portrait? I did not need to wait any longer than the first parent-teacher conference to find out. I will never forget that day. (I hope)

Sarah and her mother entered the room first. I greeted them both with a warm smile, reserving a healthy hug for Sarah. All was well until

Sarah's father entered the room. I think a video camera would have surely caught the immediate visible stiffening of his loved ones bodies. Backbones straightened and faces pinched. Sarah stopped cold, as if on alert. Her father politely shook my hand, introduced himself, and sat down next to Sarah's mother who had a nervous look in her darting eyes. Now then, I could just be super-sensitive. You be the judge. What happened next explained to me why my little Sarah had no face.

The father took the lead and wanted to know what Sarah was accomplishing. (Remember, she was in preschool where we do not always speak in terms of accomplishments.) He was very eager to share with me that he was highly educated and gifted in many of life's finest skills. He knew lots of things and was eager to "teach" them all to me. Was Sarah behaving well? Did Sarah participate in class? Was her seatwork up to snuff? Did he need to enforce any performance at home? My head was swimming. All the while, Sarah's mother sat quietly by her husband's side, face ashen, nervously picking her nails. Sarah played quietly on the corner rug, slightly rocking on her folded knees. I do not remember what I said. I assured Mr. Perfect that Sarah was a model student. I produced her best papers and discussed test results that supported her developmental adequacy. We said good-bye and shook hands. I think Sarah's mother managed to thank me. On the way out the door, the father of the year commented that I could call him any time if Sarah was not performing at peak speed. That would happen when all of the stars collided and the world ended. Just at the last second, Sarah ran into my arms for a farewell hug. I held her a few seconds longer than usual. This day, I stroked her face and told her I loved her. After they left, the room became silent, and I felt like I had been punched in the stomach.

In case you did not know, this story is a non-example of love. Some of you may have had a similar experience. I am so sorry. Just walk with me a moment while I share a secret with you. Hear this, dear sister. Take it into your heart. Drink it in. You not only should be loved, you deserve it. As surely as you are a creation of a Holy God, you are worthy to be loved.

God's Love Mends a Broken Heart

It is not a news flash that I know something about you. You are, right now, listing the reasons that you are different from Sarah and are really not all that wounded. Oh yes, you can conjure up all kinds of sympathy for that little, four-year-old, but you cannot identify. You are not worthy. If the tears have begun to settle around your lashes, it is a sign that your soul is injured and needs to be healed. It is a sign that you are dying from a lack of love. It is a sign of a broken heart.

Here is THE definition of love, from the book of 1 Corinthians 13:4-8:

> Love suffers long and is kind; love does not envy; love does not parade itself, is not puffed up; does not behave rudely, does not seek its own, is not provoked, thinks no evil; does not rejoice in iniquity, but rejoices in truth; bears all things, believes all things, hopes all things, endures all things. Love never fails.

Is Loving Easy?

We could just play a little game to see how many of the properties of love Sarah's father violated. Perhaps, you could echo the score sheet in your own father-daughter relationship. Do you still believe that you are all that different from Sarah? Please just humor me and entertain the possibility that you deserve the same sympathy as that sweet child deserved. If you were really honest, you would have to replace the word sympathy with empathy because you were there once, too. You were the invisible child. It was you rocking on your heels. It was your father dancing to his own fiddle and completely missing the beautiful music that was you. Surely, you can see that, if I know about this deep wound, it was not you. It *was* him. I often use specific terminology when I explain this kind of selfish behavior. I like to say that these kinds of dads are head-over-heels in love with themselves and cannot spare any more emotion for us. Of course, it is much more complex than this. There is a real self-esteem issue involved. But again, I am not the doctor, just the messenger.

Now then, just to be fair, it is important to accept the fact that we are all working on being better lovers. A favorite psychologist of mine was Dr. Leo Buscaglia. He actually taught his university students and his many admirers how to be better at loving each other. It is a very basic need for all of us. But, it is so-o-o hard to stay focused. I'm often so busy worrying about me that I forget about you. That's just honesty. I am an imperfect and sinful being. Now you know why I spend so much time in the woodshed with Father. By the way, this bad behavior is not an acceptable excuse for failing to love according to the rules in 1st Corinthians. Your dad either gave up early on or never tried. But, you can resolve to love others on that higher level. Look at all of the experience you have explaining to your teddy bear how you would treat others better than your crummy old dad did. Thank God for Teddy Bears!

God's Love Is the Love You Need

Hopefully, by now you are recognizing a theme. That theme is of utmost importance to your survival. I want you to develop a stubborn resolve. The worst thing you can do is to allow the sadness or regret to immobilize you into depression. You are stronger than that. I'm sure of that last statement because you have already survived using the best techniques you could discern. Likely, the rest of the world would never know, from day to day, what a wreck you are! So, you are an accomplished actress and a strong-willed girl. I invite you to use that stubbornness to propel you to positive action. You need and deserve to be loved. Your dad did not care about your need or know how to meet it. How can you survive that? Be brave. I know how.

I really want to emphasize one point first. This is a sadly *limited* list of a daughter's needs. These things are basic. Daughters also need good girlfriends, comfortable shoes, hugs, encouragement, cute hair bands, giggle time, godly counsel, spiritual food, alone time, to be trusted and admired, hobbies, a good education, respect, joy, advice, and hundreds of other things. Each of you will have your own peculiar list. Some of our lists are more peculiar than others. (Just a joke.) The point for emphasis is that God's love is the pivot from which you perform. A little girl who feels deeply loved can do all things. I really believe it. And, conversely, a little girl who was raised and lived in the love-starved desert will be unable to achieve anything. Our Father in Heaven wants you to be all that you can be and receive all that He has for you. That He is sovereign assures your receipt of these gifts. And so, you might as well get on with it. Surrender to His will and follow my next recipe.

The First Fruits Go To God

All of the loving moments that you need are right in front of your face or, at least, at your fingertips. In fact, there is a great gospel song that says it better than I can: "Loving God, loving each other, making music with my friends." Now, you may not be a student of music or performance. Nevertheless, the idea is viable. Start this way: tomorrow morning, begin your day with devotions. If you are in the middle of a sad cycle, start small. Pray a few sentences. Make sure that the first few sentences are statements of gratitude to God for His character or His provision. Ask for help and go on with your day. Do this every morning. This is called giving your first fruits to God. My husband taught me this. Did I remember to tell you how awesome he is? Anyway, expand this time with longer prayers and a little reading of His Word. Additionally, you might read a devotional or inspirational book. Write a few things down when you feel better. Make a list of to-dos for the day or make a journal entry. And, here is a really great idea. Make a list of the kind of things you need in your life to feel loved and appreciated. Be really specific. List things like: I want someone to notice my hair or I need a hug or I desire for someone to really listen to my ideas today. Keep going as long as you wish. Okay. Now, take your list and jot down the name of someone who could provide this for you, today. I am sure you can think of a teacher, pastor, friend, or co-worker who has these skills. Do you have a family member who specializes in positive feedback? Is your mother still amazed by your ability to arrange flowers? Can your pastor point you to a scripture that will provide comfort or a warm fuzzy feeling? This is important. Do not pass this off as silly. Get your daily dose of love from the people Father God has placed along side of you. And, if you still need to feel like someone loves you, get a copy of Mel Gibson's, The Passion and watch it. That should do it. By the way, I love you. Those are not just empty words either, because I *am* you. I do feel your pain. You provide the alto to my soprano as we both sing the same sad song. I found this in God's Word on an especially difficult day:

> Fear not, for I am with you;
> Be not dismayed, for I am your God.
> I will strengthen you,
> Yes, I will help you,
> I will uphold you with My righteous right hand. (Isaiah 41:10)

Upheld By His Righteous Hand

See? Those of us, who do not feel loved or loveable, feel increasingly lonely. We feel abandoned. We are afraid that it will never change. It becomes a self-compounding sentence with no chance for parole. And so, when I read this verse, I was immediately filled with hope. I wonder if you keyed on the same part of the verse that I did. I was especially comforted by the promise that Abba Father would uphold me with His hand. The simple extension of a comforting and safe hand means something to a wounded child. And, if you have studied The Bible, you know that the Father's right hand has special significance. This is where Jesus sits. I'll illustrate further.

Have you ever seen the Mr. Magoo version of *The Christmas Carol*? There is a soulful little song sung by young Ebenezer Scrooge as he deals with his own unhappy youth. He sings: "A hand for each hand was planned for the world. Why won't my fingers reach? Millions of grains of sand in the world. Why such a lonely beach?" The last line of the song is: "I'm all alone in the world." Growing up in a tentative world gives us a great understanding for this kind of pathos. You and I know that when you are loved, those who love you adore your company. And, we believe that our dad did not want to be with us because he did not love us. It may have been true. Still, this whole business of having a hand to hold speaks to the core of our most painful beliefs. A mother holding your hand as you cross a busy street means love. A friend holding your hand as you get your ears pierced means love. A husband holding your hand while you give birth means love. And, a father holding your hand after a bad dream means love. Our Father in Heaven loves us. Do you know how I know? He said:

> For I, the Lord your God, will hold your right hand,
> Saying to you, 'Fear not, I will help you.' (Isaiah 41:13)

Now, that's love. A daughter needs that.

I hope you will gather love into your life in every way possible. Mostly, I hope you will grab onto the Lord's right hand and trust His promises. Love is an experience. We were born knowing need. We learned about love. It's time to get an advanced degree from Dad. (You know Who I mean.)

It is entirely possible to discuss these vital topics in a more exhaustive manner. I just do not think you need more discussion, because you have been longing for these answers for a long time. So, I know we can go on to the next level. This one may sound annoying. But, stay alert. The subject may take a turn.

What Does God Expect From Us?

Let's talk about the responsibilities of a daughter. God's Word leaves no stone unturned. Often, when Father is speaking about our responsibilities, it is not an either/or scenario or even a you go first/ I'll follow situation. I'm thinking about such scripture as:

> Wives, submit to your own husbands as to the Lord.
> Husbands, love your wives just as Christ loved the
> Church, and gave Himself for her... (Ephesians 5:22-25)

We tend not to like it very much. By the way, that whole submitting part comes first in the book. And yes, I have heard all of the rationalizations. But, I digress. We are discussing your responsibilities as a daughter. Now the pointer is positioned in the opposite direction, so stand up tall. We want to give ourselves every advantage.

I'm going to take a stab in the dark and guess that not all of your days growing up were filled with eyelet dresses, humble, down-turned eyes, and obedient smiles. If I know you as I think I do, once in a while you donned a raggedy pair of jeans, stared with defiance into the eyes of an unreasonable or cruel father, or even spit venom through tight lips. Sometimes, it is a matter of survival to leave behind the gentle arts. Don't think that I stand in judgment at whatever you had to do to survive. I do not. You see, I was a really frightened child. My survival technique was to curl up in a nondiscernable ball in my bedroom closet. It seldom worked. By the way, today I am claustrophobic. Closets scare me.

To continue, even in the most simple of relationships there is a responsibility for an exchange. That is how we loosely define a relationship, one organism acting upon another. We're going to stick to human relationships here, so don't get philosophical on me.

The Bible says that we are to love God with all our heart, might, mind, and strength. As you know, our God does not stop there. He continues with this gem: "Love thy neighbor as thyself." Or, we could ask ourselves about this one: "Love one another as I have loved you." I sense trouble brewing, but I think we have come so far together, that you are going to be just fine.

It will probably come as no surprise to you that parents share many of the needs of a daughter. They need the same stuff. They are usually anesthetized to that fact. That just means they are asleep and need to be awakened. Do not despair that I have forgotten the possibility that your dad deserves nothing from you. Too horrible to imagine are the life's experiences that come from an abusive home. I pray that, in some way, you will heal and get past these awful events. They serve no useful purpose today.

How Christians Glorify God

So, if you are a Believer, it is time to be about your Father's business. It is time for you to focus on becoming more like Christ and fulfilling the purpose for which you were created. And, like the catechism response that my husband teaches in our Christian school says: "You were created to glorify God and enjoy Him forever." I don't know about you, but I've got work to do. Let's explore some of the stumbling blocks that may be keeping you from gaining this full fellowship with Father God.

In our childcare, we try very hard to teach the children to be responsible. When they take out a toy, they must put it back before getting another. If they make a mistake, they must confess and apologize. Restitution is also encouraged. We teach the children to be honest. In fact, the kids know that if they make a mistake, I will most certainly forgive them if they are truthful about it. Conversely, if they make a mistake and lie about it, I will not hold back the floodgates of consequences. It is not pretty. Our staff is trained to present snacks, treats and meals in a structured manner that requires the child to clean up his or her own mess. They ask to be excused from the table. Little girls are seated first. They are also served first. That is the tip of the proverbial iceberg. You get the point. We train children to be responsible so that they will be good mommies and daddies and so that our world will be a better place. We seek success for our kids. We do not settle for mediocre or lazy accomplishments. Our motto is: High expectations for behavior—low tolerance for failure. Does that sound harsh? Remember, that I truly love children, and so, all of these things are taught *in love*. A favorite quote of mine is this: "If a child is not disciplined, with love, by his tiny world, he will be disciplined, without love, by the larger one." We do not just take up space and breathe the air, here. We have responsibilities. God has a plan and expectations for His kids. Often, we are curious about the plan and, like my students, not so enthusiastic about the expectations. Father God plans for us to glorify Him in our lives. Tell me. If someone were to secretly film your day, would they see you glorifying God? Or, would your plan not include that lofty of a criterion? Use your plan or use Father's. But remember, God's plan is a perfect plan that will lead us home.

By now, I hope you are comfortable with your responsibilities. I'd like to share a suggested list of them with you, if you are ready. If you are not, go and get a cookie and come back when you feel stronger.

How to Accomplish God's Calling on Your Life

Daughters should honor their fathers and mothers that their days may be long upon the earth. Oh, boy. I can feel you shaking your head, now. Maybe, even some of you are just plain shaking, either with anger or sadness. Get the woobie and listen to the last part of that commandment. Yes, I did say commandment. It is not a suggestion. Our Father in Heaven expects you to honor those who participated in your birth. I'll redeem myself soon, so don't go away. You know, by now, that I am not so dumb that I expect you to approve of the ungodly things that your dad may have perpetrated against you. You also know that I do not want you in harm's way ever again. If your earthly father was this caliber of fellow, keep away. You are perfectly within God's will to turn from evil in all of its forms. Think about finding someone else to look up to. You might try developing a similar relationship with a pastor, teacher, or friend. As members of the body of Christ, we are to lift each other up. Seek high caliber Christians for this job.

However, if your childhood was difficult and tenuous, but your father was not one of these monsters, you have much to do. You must first strengthen yourself for the battle. Gaining ground in this relationship will not be easy. You have regrets, fears, and un-met needs. Just entertain the possibility that your dad does, too. You may never hear those words from his lips. My dad never said them. I only want you to remember that you are the special child of a Mighty God who can do all things. Breathe in. Breathe out.

Now, think about ways you could re-formulate your father-daughter relationship. Is your father still running from you? Don't chase him. Send cards or e-mail. Remember his birthday. Tell your kids about the hamburger gravy he made when your mother was away. Yes, my dad did just that and I am still not sure what he was thinking. Apparently, when my father was in the army, this was perfectly acceptable "grub." A-k-k-k!

Emotional House Cleaning

Look closely at your own behavior and change what you find that hearkens back to him. Revenge is for The Lord, but His revenge is not heaped upon you in the form of your similarities to your dad. My cynical little daughter struggles with this mistaken belief.

God chastens those He loves but *truly* punishes His enemies. He knows what is best. I'm suggesting that you get to know your dad as he is now. I bet his hair is gray or gone. I bet he isn't as strong as he used to be. I bet he may even be lonely. We both know that he doesn't exactly stimulate fellowship in others. Sister, when you are really feeling stronger, genuinely try to understand him. How often in your life have you known someone and not cared to associate with him or her until you found the reason for his or her bad behavior and felt sympathy? Even if all you ever feel for your dad is sympathy, it is much better and much less personally destructive than hatred.

In the last eight years of my father's life, as he struggled with a horrifically debilitating stroke, I came to appreciate his life and his struggle. He was often moved to tears whenever I visited him. He was gentle and humble. He was helpless and depressed. I was overwhelmed with sorrow for his condition. All of the anger melted away as I watched his suffering. You see, we all come to our own Calvary at some point in our lives and who is to say which one of us was the most sinful? I wish I could have honored him more. I was not a good daughter. Take a lesson.

And so, we are responsible as daughters to grow up and forgive. We are required to be like Jesus in the lives of others. We are to glorify God in all that we do. This earth is not our home. It is just a brief stop. It will comfort you to learn to live a Christian life in which you honor your father the best that you can. I know you will come up with something. By the way, after a time of trying this, see if a real healing has just sneaked up on you and the burden is lifted.

Using Your God-given Gifts

If honoring our parents were our only responsibility, it would still be a life's accomplishment. But, by now you know that I have more to discuss. Daughters must also share their gifts and, in so doing, honor their Father God. Okay. Okay. Stop rolling your eyes! I know the topic of individual gifts really irritates many of us. I can't tell you how many times I have been seated across from a dear sister in the Lord as she firmly confessed to an absence of personal gifts. The truth is almost as disheartening.

Looking to God for Strength

Remember when we began our journey and I expressed my concern about your self-identity? I said that I did not think you know who you are. Hopefully, that vision is becoming clear because it is impossible to see a positive character trait or *gift* when you are busily engaged in self-loathing or hyper-vigilant self-protection. O-o-o-o, the big words are rollin'. I just mean that if you hate yourself or live with constant fear, it is difficult to assess your dynamic abilities. Most often, your time is filled with hiding your true feelings and a shy acceptance of your lack. Oh, by the way, I have seen this particular problem present in another way. Some of us (guilty, as charged) over-compensate for our low self-esteem and fear-filled lives by showing off or becoming highly educated to throw folks off our trail. It is really the same end result. Little girls who were discouraged early on think of themselves as examples of wasted lives, un-loveable, and limited in desirable traits. You will demean your gifts in conversations with others, play down your talents, or volley back the compliments lest someone think you are truly worthwhile. Phrases like: "Oh, this old thing," or "Anyone could have done this," are part and parcel of your daily interactions with others. It is time to throw off the old habits and begin again on the path of self-discovery. Take this responsibility seriously. The sovereign Lord of the universe does. He said you were created *for such a time as this* and *for good works*. Don't forget we are to be about the business of glorifying and enjoying Him. You cannot glorify the One who offers you such amazing love if you will not look up in hope. During a vicious storm, Peter the Apostle lost hope and was really sunk! And then the very *second* he placed his trust in Jesus, he was saved from drowning. You are a precious child with a great work to do in your Father's Name. Let's get to it. You may be sinking fast.

Hiding Your Light

I was asked one time by a neighbor of mine how I managed to do so many things so well. I said: "Oh, you haven't seen my closets!" She laughed. I laughed, politely. And, I continued the performance. You've already guessed that I meant that statement. My closets were (are) a nightmare. I've already shared with you that as a small child during many fearful times, I hid out in my closet. Until I understood the great love God has for me, I stayed in that closet with all of its ghosts and kept others out. No one was allowed in there but me. I mean *no one*. It is surprising how easy it is to fool others into believing that you have it all together. Well, I guess I did have it all together. I just kept it in the dark spaces, hidden from view. I suspect that you may see yourself in this story. At least, I hope you do so that I am not the only nut cake on the shelf.

I wish I could report that I had a sudden realization or an inspiration one day and just came out of my closet. It was not that way at all. What really happened was a God-thing. How grateful I am to Father that He does not save us and forget us. The Good Shepherd is not going to spend all of that time looking for a lost sheep only to allow it to spend the rest of its fuzzy, little life eating bad grass and hanging out with the troubled of the flock. He comes to get you and He begins a work that He is always faithful to complete.

To Effect a Change

And so, after I became a Christian, God saw to it that His message to me was clear and repetitive. I can never seem to get anything on the first time. I need repetition. I need repetition. (Silly) True to His promise, our Father in Heaven found my soft spot. Since gospel music is such a delight to my soul, that's where God began to train me. I first heard the song, "Search Me." If you have not heard it, I recommend the Cathedral's version. That song got me thinking that perhaps there were some things in my heart that I did not fully understand and may not want to keep. I thought if God did the choosing, surely I could keep what was good and discard what was not. But you know, God is smarter than me. He knew what was in there, and

He knew I was the one to do the house cleaning. So, He sent me another song: "Change My Heart, O God." I will often sing these anointed words whenever I am a little off track.

> Change my heart, O God. Make it ever true.
> Change my heart, O God. May I be like You.
>
> You are the Potter. I am the clay.
> Mold me and make me. This is what I pray.
>
> Change my heart, O God. Make it ever true.
> Change my heart, O God. May I be like You.

If that does not get to you and send a little shiver of concern up your spine, you are not who I think you are. I might suggest a note of caution here. Please do not graduate to singing "Refiner's Fire" until you are really ready for the heat! God will not hold back this gift!

Doing God's Will in Your Life

And so, I began my search. As I was cleaning closets and wincing at the things I found, one question kept running through my mind. With all of this ugliness hidden in my heart, why in the world did God even want me in His kingdom? Was He crazy? He had millions to choose from, and He chose me. What was going on here? And then, it struck me. All things came together for the first time. Father *knew* me. He created me and He loved me, anyway. I finally understood that He had a job for me to do. Now a new heart *cannot* turn from the Father. We are His, no matter what. It will only prolong things for you to ignore this message. God has a plan for your life.(Sound familiar?) He made the plan and now you must work the plan. I'm going to give you big hints now.

When God created you, He had in mind what the course of your life would be. He watches you as it unfolds and guides each step, places desires in your heart, and predestines your joys, your learning experiences, and your gifts. He *will* have His way with you. In the most glorious manner imaginable, Father God has begun this loving work. He has ordained the privilege of discovery for each of His children. With that in your heart, let us begin.

How to Find Your Gifts

What do you love, deeply? What makes you joyful? Is there something that you seem to be able to do quite well? What is it that seems to be a running theme in your life? For me, it seemed that no matter where I was, children were there. Every job I ever had entailed working with kids. Every event I attended, I gravitated to the kids. I mean, I got down on the ground, looked at bugs, and held real conversations about glue. It was fun! Is there some recurring theme in your life? Do you know what it is? Think about it because, chances are, that is a message from God. You just need to fine-tune the gift and use it to glorify Him. Please generate your own list. Yes, I said list. You may have more than one talent or gift. To help get you started, consider these:

    the gift of organization,
    the gift of kindness,
    the gift of music,
    the gift of supporting a good work,
    the gift of laughter,
    the gift of compassion,
    the gift of cheerful conversation,
    the gift of homemaking,
    the gift of cooking,
    the gift of speaking,
    the gift of accounting,
    the gift of understanding,
    the gift of patience,
    the gift of a green thumb,
    the gift of charity,
    the gift of empathy,
    the gift of flower arranging,
    the gift of cleaning,
    the gift of service,
    the gift of teaching,
    the gift of evangelization,
    the gift of reading,
    the gift of sharing,
    the gift of drawing,
    the gift of caring for the sick, elderly or young,
    the gift of shopping (Yeah!),
    the gift of managing a business,
    the gift of managing your children,
    the gift of constructive conversation,
    the gift of problem solving,
    the gift of creativity,
    the gift of frugality,
    the gift of writing,
    the gift of building,

the gift of mechanical skill,
the gift of forgiveness,
the gift of peace,
the gift of adventure,
the gift of courage,
the gift of arbitration,
the gift of entertaining,
the gift of handiwork,
the gift of gardening,
the gift of defending the weak,
the gift of physical strength,
the gift of counseling,
the gift of dreaming,
the gift of making soap,
the gift of financial astuteness,
the gift of bringing out the best in others,
the gift of display,
the gift of helpfulness,
the gift of gift-giving,
the gift of decorating, or
the gift of discernment.

I could go on into my eternal rest and still not cover the topic, exhaustively. Anyway, you know what yours are. Tip over that bushel basket and let your light shine. I'm excited to see what you will do. But, do not forget that it is your responsibility to begin to work God's plan for your life. A good daughter will develop all of her talents and glorify her Father.

From Giving Comes Reconciliation

Well now, how *does* this fit in with the duties you may have pertaining to *your* dad? I don't know. But, you do. If your relationship with your father is salvageable, something on your gift list will improve his life and yours. He may need your encouragement, today. He may wish to see you smile, today. He may need you to run a few errands. He may want your opinion about some little thing. He may need some of your time. He may need a haircut. He may need a new shirt. He may need a ride. He may need to know that you are thinking about him. Hold on. He may need your forgiveness and final peace. Do unto others is not just a cute saying. It may sting a little, but the healing will be apparent in your singing soul. I think I can leave you here for a few minutes. Come back when you are ready to go on.

Sanctification as a Process

As daughters, we are responsible for our own actions and responses. We are required not to play the blame game in an unholy way. I want you to understand the difference between holding someone accountable for their actions and blaming your failures on another. Too many of us carry the open wounds from childhood sadness into our own adult lives and never reach our full potential. I know of fifty and sixty-year-old folks who are still blaming their parents for their tempers, or their drinking, or their philandering. That just sounds silly when it is on paper. Surely, no one is that dense. I know I was. Until I was forty, I was convinced that my bad relationships were the fault of a distant and non-affectionate father. If only he had hugged me or noticed me or encouraged me, maybe I would have chosen my companions more wisely. Oh, please! Now that may sound harsh, but remember, I am speaking to myself here. If you relate, then read on bravely. I'm not finished. In fact, none of us are finished. Our sanctification is a process and a work orchestrated by God that lasts a lifetime, even an eternity. Unfortunately, that does not let us off the hook today.

How to Use Your Gifts to Glorify God

Up to now, the concept of inheritance has been understood as those gifts or traits given to us by our predecessors. We, of course, have been trying to understand how we fit into God's family and what He expects of us in return. If we are to live as joint-heirs with Christ, it makes sense for us to begin seriously attempting to achieve personal perfection. No. I have not gone over the edge. We are Father's creation and will never reach the level of perfection to which He holds Himself. Nevertheless, The Bible instructs us to put on the whole counsel of God. We are children of The Promise who, with the strength of God, must stand on our own feet with renewed resolve to honor and glorify our Maker. You are responsible for your actions and reactions. The seeds that you sow will reap rewards. These may not always be happy rewards. But, be assured that you *will* reap what you sow. The Father up above will not be so interested in why you are the way you are as He is in what you do with what you have. He knows why you are the way you are because He created you that way. So, you must be about the business of using your gifts to lift up His name in all the earth. If your earthly father impedes this progress, cut him from the herd. Choose other mentors. Get up, get real, and get glorifying, because it is now your move.

The Results of Persecution

I suppose that you can now understand why the students at our Christian school do not like to spend time in the office with me. I am simply no-nonsense when it comes to conduct and accomplishments. I don't have time to play Dr. Phil when such eternal concepts are at risk. Sure, you have been abused. Yes, I am saddened by your story. But, I want you to have peace and feel success outside of that sadness. I know that you will begin a new and fulfilling life if you heed these words. Perhaps the book of Job can convince you. I cannot think of another account in all of God's Word that is a more complete commentary on the persecuted life, save the account of the ministry of Jesus Christ. I would never desire to mitigate the many sacrifices and countless persecutions suffered by the apostles and disciples, early Christians, or today's persecuted church. By now, I hope you know that I appreciate *your* pain, also. But, just for the sake of comparison, let's return to Job. He says:

> For I know that my Redeemer lives,
> And He shall stand at last on the earth;
> And after my skin is destroyed, this I know,
> That in my flesh I shall see God,
> Whom I shall see for myself,
> And my eyes shall behold, and not another.
> How my heart yearns within me! (Job 19: 25-27)

Job knew that Father was to be ultimately trusted in His promises to deliver His children from all manner of evil. Like Paul, Job understood that nothing could be perpetrated against the body that would not point the true Believer to His Savior and the promise of eternal joy. As the great Apostle Paul said: *"For to me, to live is Christ, and to die is gain."* (Phil.1:21) That's what the man said even as he suffered persecution after persecution. Like Job, Paul stood fast. Both knew that this earth was not their home and that God would come for them soon.

What Is A Redeemer?

But, look carefully at the previous scripture. Did you know that the Hebrew word "Redeemer" might also be rendered "Avenger", "Vindicator", or "Kinsman-Redeemer?" You could ask Ruth about that when you see her. Without her kinsman-redeemer, the lineage of our Savior would not have included her name. Without ours, we would not be going home at all.

Finally, guess what we can learn from reading about Job? He was like the country music song, played backward. He got his family back. He got his wealth back. He got his position back. He got his friends back. God *heaped* blessings upon him. Staying the course can be very beneficial and, in eternal terms, it is our only hope.

The Process of Healing

Well, sister, there is something you must understand before we go on. There may never be a day that you look around and, with a sigh of relief, are completely healed. To help you ride out the storms, let's talk about an emotional process common to the human condition. Because this is an imperfect and decaying world, everyone on it will suffer setbacks, difficulties, injuries, sorrows, disappointments, and calamities. That list will most certainly not ever show up on a Hallmark card. However, we do have similar experiences and can learn from each other. There is an old saying that if we ignore historical events, we are doomed to repeat them. There is another one about experience being a harsh teacher. Choose the one you like best and understand this concept: We all live on the same planet, have been created by the same God, and will deal with the same earthly encounters.

Paul, the apostle, who came into the service of the Lord after an ignoble career of persecuting Christians, knew much about grief and sorrow. We relate to his suffering as he said: *"We are hard-pressed on every side, yet not crushed; we are perplexed, but not in despair; persecuted but not forsaken, struck down, but not destroyed."* (2nd Cor. 4:8-9) And again, we empathize when he explains his own mournful feelings with such hope saying: *"For our light affliction, which is but for a moment, is working for us a far more exceeding and eternal weight of glory, while we do not look at the things which are seen, but at the things which are not seen. For the things which are seen are temporary, but the things which are not seen are eternal."* (2nd Cor. 4:17-18) Paul goes on to explain "groaning" in our own skin, and the final victory in eternity. I think he knew from grief and sadness. With that foundation, stick with me while I help you to understand why this is important.

The Grieving Process

When something really awful happens to us, we often share common experiences. These experiences are so universal that many theories have been advanced to explain the phenomenon. You may have heard this model referred to as the Mourning Process. If you are well read, you will recognize the work of Elisabeth Kubler-Ross in her theory of The Stages of Grief.

Many more have theorized about this concept, re-arranged or abridged some of it, and written lots of books on the subject. Suffice to say that there are many similarities in each model and again, I am not a psychologist nor am I here to play doctor, so you and I will just take a look at the basics. Ms. Kubler-Ross proposes that when something bad happens to you, you will go through the following stages:

1. Denial and isolation
2. Anger
3. Bargaining
4. Depression
5. Acceptance

This particular work focused on the bereavement process or how we experience the loss of a loved one. The beauty of this is that it can apply to many of life's challenges from the birth of a disabled or sick child to the loss of your own health and even include the separation of death. I remember a particularly dark time in my dad's life after he suffered his first debilitating stroke. He lost the sight in his right eye except for a little circle of sight in the center, a kind of window. He had been an avid golfer all of his life and probably the most independent man I ever knew. My dad was a formidable force who broadcast self-assurance like an air-raid siren. But after this stroke, he sat dejected and demoralized in his favorite chair convinced that he would never drive a car or a golf ball again. Now, I am a little bit of a non-conformist, as you know. And, I began thinking: how could we restore some of my father's normal life to him? I had an idea. Initially, I did not think it would work. Nonetheless, I got into my car, closed my right eye and drove three miles to his house, unintentionally winking at all of the other drivers on the road. That must have been a sight. The good news was that I made it and even learned that it was not all that hard. Only my depth perception had suffered somewhat so dad will never know how endangered his garage door was that day. I marched into his sitting room like the conquering hero and announced my findings to his majesty. He seemed un-impressed and responded in a nonchalant manner. It was only a few days before he was driving and golfing again. It probably was not my goofy stunt that convinced him. But, it illustrates the point.

When bad things happen, we go through similar feelings. Dad had isolated himself. He was angry. Though he never told me this, I'm sure he tried to convince God that he needed another chance and would make good on that chance. I know he was depressed. He just sat and sat. However, in this case, his acceptance of his circumstance allowed him to go on and live with fullness for several more years. You can do this with many things. Even the worst situations may have hopeful outcomes. As Paul concluded: *"I have fought the good fight, I have finished the race, I have kept the faith. Finally, there is laid up for me the crown of righteousness, which the Lord, the righteous Judge, will give to me on that Day, and not to me only but also to all who have loved His appearing."* (2nd Tim.4:7-8) The day will come for you, too.

Now, you may be hoping that the stages of grief, as presented, are like a road map or a recipe. You know, it is always comforting to have some control over bad things. If you have ever given birth, it is nice to know that the pain will eventually end, you will live, and a baby will be going home with you. Those facts help us to tolerate the worst pain imaginable. I apologize that this is not one of those faithful promises. You see, grief is experienced differently by each of us. The stages may be out of order or move in slow motion as you get stuck on one or the other. Or, just as you believe that you have recovered somewhat from your loss and reached the stage of acceptance, a sight, a smell, a sound sends you twirling back to stage one or raging into stage two. And, the whole process begins anew.

In his book, *Good Grief,* G.E. Westberg presents ten stages in the grieving process. His model looks like this:

1. We are in a state of shock.
2. We express emotion.
3. We feel depressed and very lonely.
4. We experience physical symptoms.
5. We may become panicky.
6. We feel a sense of guilt about the loss.
7. We are filled with anger and resentment.
8. We resist returning.
9. Gradually hope comes through.
10. We struggle to affirm reality.

Wow. Did you know that so much was happening? I don't think we really recognize anything except the *anguish* of loss or disappointment and fear during the low times of our life. What I want you to take away from this discussion is a sure knowledge that all of us, at one time or another, have been there. We all suffer. We all mourn.

Bad Things Happen to Bad People

Where am I going with this? Sadly, I grew up believing that something was very wrong with me because I could not seem to stimulate gentleness, fondness, and love in my dad's heart toward me. I kept trying to figure out what I was doing wrong. As a mixed-up teenager, I chose to blame him for being a lousy father. I had lots of creative ways to express this. I would never use those words today to refer to anyone, let alone my father. As I look back, a more mature reason provides an adequate explanation for my dad's behavior. It really wasn't me. It really was my dad. But, even as a young adult with a child of my own, I was still carrying resentment toward him for not parenting me the right way. I was angry from lack of affection. I was blaming and punitive. I just could not grow up. Then, I came upon the concept of the grieving process. It was another installment in God's training program. I did not know I would need to understand this, but Father did. Just consider this possibility. You must grieve the loss of your childhood. You must mourn the absence of a loving daddy. You must suffer the pain of unmet needs and unfulfilled dreams. You've got to cry it out or scream it out or talk it out or, better still, pray it out. I write this book to help you work it out. Because until you let your dad or yourself or your miserable mom off the hook, you will not focus on what is important and get on with your life. Drugs, alcohol, sexual sin, tranquilizers, food, work, spending, gambling, and thousands of other wasteful things will become your coping mechanisms.

God's Grace is Sufficient

You can blame your father, or your lost youth, or your bad luck for every failure you have met. That is not the mark of a victorious life. That is not what your Abba Father has planned for you. The very difficulties and trials that hold your soul hostage are the things that will give you strength in the future. How do I know this? I know this because the apostle Paul presented the case for The Lord, Jesus in 2nd Corinthians 12:9 when he wrote: *"And he said unto me; My grace is sufficient for thee, for my strength is made perfect in weakness. Most gladly therefore will I rather glory in my infirmities, that the power of Christ may rest upon me."* I know Paul was really something. I may not ever be that strong and faithful as to glory in my infirmities. But, we need to be reminded that sometimes Father puts us in a hiding place as we await our Heavenly inheritance. 1st Peter 1:6-9 says it like this: *"In this you greatly rejoice, though now, for a little while, if need be, you have been grieved by various trials, that the genuineness of your faith, being much more precious than gold that perishes, though it is tested by fire, may be found to praise, honor, and glory at the revelation of Jesus Christ, whom having not seen you love. Though now you do not see Him, yet believing, you rejoice with joy inexpressible and full of glory, receiving the end of your faith---the salvation of your souls."*

It is a test worth passing. Even the great prophet Elijah had to suffer a time of waiting planned by God and catered by a flock of birds. You *need* Jesus, precious one. Cast your burdens upon Him and even as Simon of Cyrene carried the crucifixion tree up the last hill, Jesus will lift you up and carry you home.

As a final consideration of this context, I invite you to reflect on this very astute observation. This illustration is not mine. I apologize that I cannot remember its author. Nevertheless, it is pure gold. Imagine if you will, a boat as it leaves port to sail out to sea. At one end, loved ones are waving goodbye in sad acceptance of the inevitable separation, but as the ship crosses the horizon, there on the other shore with arms lifted in greeting, stand souls joyful at the arrival. As you leave behind your regrets and shattered dreams, before you shines the light of a new day made just for you. Love, Father God.

The Peace of Full Reconciliation

How lovely it would be to sit back now and rest in this peaceful and hopeful circumstance. It may be the first time in years that you have felt like your next day might not be so bad. In fact, you may be looking forward to tomorrow and new challenges. I wish I could pat you on the back and send you on your way. But, you know better. I'm going to expect something from you and it probably won't be easy. You are correct, and I have an assignment for you. At the end of this time of learning comes your greatest task of all—reconciliation. We have to explore it because God has commanded it. He wants all of His children to revel in the peace of mind that comes from having no regrets. And so, I want you to learn how to do it. Take your fingers out of your ears, because you can't fool me. I think, on some level, you desire this peace. Let us begin to appreciate this vital concept.

To reconcile: "To cease hostility or opposition, to restore or make good again, also to regain communion." I think we may have a three-step process here. The only prerequisite to a better understanding is whether or not you are ready to take these particular three steps. Luckily, I know what to do. I want you to take a moment to run a little inventory. This activity will be a little harder than organizing your sock drawer, though that can certainly be an exercise in self-control. (P.S.: Why do I always cling to my high-school knee-highs, when I no longer have high school knees? And, what is the deal with my fear of tossing out old nylons? I do not have time to stuff a pillow, make a puppet, or rob a bank. Are you out there, my people?)

Biblical Principles Will Guide You

To get back on track, we must now focus on your intimate and personal beliefs. Even though I have been in similar emotional territory, your feelings and thoughts are unique. So, I can make suggestions, but you must do most of the work. Sound familiar? Anyway, I want you to be really honest with yourself as you look at your belief systems, especially as they relate to your relationships. I know we all come into any relationship with certain expectations. That's okay if those expectations are in line with good, sound, Biblical principles. Our Father in Heaven wisely expects you to spend your time with other Believers who love The Lord and seek to do His Will. The short circuit occurs when our beliefs about relationships are distorted by past failures or fears. We may even disrupt current relationships based on our memories about past ones. Either scenario spells trouble in the future. You see, memories are most often softened or just down right fabricated by our desire to wax nostalgic and, as we have already learned, fear and it's expectation of failure may leave us frozen and unable to seek new and hopeful associations. So, you have got to be brutal in this exercise in order to bring healing. I promised you that I would give you real things to *do* and not just pretty words. This is the part where you step up and take your life back because we already know what happened, what we need, and what God wants us to do. Additionally, you were given the righteous opportunity to mourn your loss and cleanse your soul. Now, you must get on with it. And, just as Esther cried as she prepared to rebelliously break the law: "*. . . .-and if I perish, I perish!*" (Esther 4:16b), we must be ready to step out in the faith that Father will lift us. Daniel, in the lion's den, stepped out into what must have seemed certain peril, and Job with passion and trembling decried: "*Why do I take my flesh I my teeth, and put my life in my hands? Though He slay me, yet I will trust Him. . . . I know that I shall be vindicated. Who is he who will contend with me? If now I hold my tongue, I perish.*" (Job 13:14-15a, 18b-19) Job knew who would rescue him. You are no less God's beloved.

Step one is to search your heart for the deep beliefs that you have. Do you believe that you are not a loveable person? Do you think you deserve to be abused? Somewhere hidden inside your soul, are you convinced of your lack of worthiness or usefulness? Are you sure that you do not have gifts to share? (Refer back to the section on a daughter's responsibilities and read it until you get it.) Do you question your intelligence or the way you process what you see? Do you think you are the only weirdo who feels like you do? Have you ever felt certifiably crazy? Do you believe that until you learn to do things the "right" way, you will continue to be unhappy? Are you dealing with honest fears connected with change? I used to imagine that if I accepted my parent's mistakes and became comfortable with my own ideas, my head would blow up. That's silly, I know. But, I sure had lots of headaches until I figured that one out. Let's continue for a few moments. Are you just certain that what you believe is what *everyone* believes? Have you ever polled some other people to see if there really is only one way to cut the pie? And now, this is really important. Is there someone in your life who will truly be honest with you about your beliefs? Are you ready to hear the truth? If you cannot say yes to the last two questions, hear this:

> Happy is the man, who finds wisdom,
> And the man who gains understanding;
> For her proceeds are better than the profits of silver,
> And her gain than fine gold.
> She is more precious than rubies,
> And all the things you may desire cannot compare with her.
> Length of days is in her right hand,
> In her left hand riches and honor.
> Her ways are ways of pleasantness,
> And all her paths are peace.
> She is a tree of life to those who take hold of her,
> And happy are all who retain her." (Proverbs 3: 13-18)

Scripture as a Measuring Stick

If you seek this wisdom, God will bless your efforts. Take a break if you need one and read lots of the book of Proverbs. If ever there were an essay on mistaken beliefs, that book fits the description. By now, most of your hostilities have ceased, if only because you have been concentrating so carefully on understanding your beliefs. In case you did not notice, you have taken control of your feelings and your future. When you feel stronger and wiser, move to step two.

You might want to grab a little paper bag now. Lots of hyperventilation occurs during this portion of the show. I'm going to ask you to examine, carefully, the beliefs that you listed. If anything sounds silly now, discard it. You do not need silly beliefs cluttering up your spiritual sock drawer. An example of a silly belief is that your head will blow up if you disagree with your parents. I can dish it *and* take it. Take the remaining beliefs and begin to explore them.

Mistaken Beliefs

Okay. I had this really neat pair of sandals when I was 18 years old. They had alternating red, white, and blue straps. They had cute, little, squared high heels. I only wore them when my outfit matched, exactly. Everything about these sandals was perfect. Did I happen to mention that the sandals in question were a petite, size 5? When I bought them, they fit just fine. Twenty-eight years later, they did not, but I still had them. Taking those sandals to goodwill was like closing the door on my youth, forever. It was like giving up a part of me. It was a miserable event. I could no longer wear them. They were outdated and ragged, but I suffered with the loss. Now it seems silly. I have other shoes. They are cool, too. What was I hanging on to? You see, those shoes held a deeper meaning for me. They meant independence, ownership, control, and the desire to "have it all together." In fact, the *shoes* meant nothing. They were just shoes. But, until I could understand that on a deep-seated level, those sandals were staying until the Day of the Lord. I gave them away when I fell in love with my husband, the pastor. I now had a wonderful husband, an awesome daughter, and a blossoming relationship with Jesus Christ. I did not need red, white, and blue sandals. How does this relate to your belief system, you ask? Once you understand what your beliefs are, you can begin to uncover the meaning that they hold. Asking why you believe goes to the core of the value of them. As you prayerfully assess the value of a belief, you can determine whether to keep it or toss it. How about another illustration?

I have a strange sense of humor. I think you have guessed by now. Often, that sense of humor is unappreciated in certain circles. Go figure. The story I want to tell is about my cute daughter, though. She *does* appreciate my silliness. However, a joke is only as good as its audience. And, her poor, little childhood was peppered with things that I thought were funny and turned out not to humor her quite as much. She tolerates me still and tells friends about her crazy mother and the tales I would tell. There was one, particular joke out of which I got a lot of mileage. We traveled by car, often, as she was growing up. On the road were lots of cargo trucks. I was often bored while riding and so stories just grew in my head that had to be told. Here comes the joke. There was a certain trucking company whose name initials were I.M.L. I don't know what that really stands for. I did not need to know to create the story. I conjured an elaborate tale about strange-looking birds called Imls with big, orange legs, fluffy bodies, and a low tolerance for the heat. I told my impressionable daughter that these birds came from the Arctic and needed to be carried in large, refrigerated trucks from zoo to zoo so that the whole world could learn about Imls.

She bought it. Later, when we visited the zoo, the most amazing pay-off occurred. We saw some large, awkward birds, called Emus and I was able to convince my sweetie that it was misspelled, but that these were the guys. She takes great joy in re-telling this story, today, so that others may know how special I am. Me-thinks she has the same gene.

The Real Work of Change

I tell you that story to help you weed out those beliefs that just do not serve you anymore. If we want to be focused on the call of The Father, unnecessary beliefs need to be released into the wild. Are you really worthless? Will the mistakes of your youth doom your future in every way? Was your dad right about you? Do you do everything wrong? If you marry the man of your dreams, will he just turn out to be like your father? If you do not worry about something, does that mean you do not care or it will never change? Are you powerless to change your life? Is fate in control of your future? If all of your plans go awry, does that make your dad right about your choices? Are you too weak to get through the day without some help? If you don't check with your mom before you make a move, will it be a mistake? If you move to a new town or start a new job, will you be sorry? If you do not experience fear with new experiences, will you do something stupid and get hurt? When you blame yourself for the things that go wrong, will you try harder in the future to do the right thing? If you never risk anything, will you be safe from losing everything? Is keeping your secret the only way to save your life? Will you die if someone finds out the truth about you? I could go on forever. Your questions are personal and deeply rooted. Be patient with yourself. I promise you that, when you ask these questions and discard those old, tired, mistaken beliefs, you can begin again. This is the part of reconciliation that makes all things new. Like a piece of classic furniture, restoration brings a new shine, a new purpose, and a new hope. It will also allow us to move on to step three. It is my wish that you are on the healing path already because, truly, the best is yet to come.

Face-to-Face With God

The prefix Pros is Greek and it means *face-to-face*. It happens to be the prefix used in the Bible in reference to our fellowship with God. I think it would be accurate to assume that your earthly father was not very good at face-to-face fellowship. I know mine was not. In fact, we had a little sarcastic joke among my teen-aged friends who knew my father. They called him "the head." This nickname had nothing to do with his intellect or the size of his skull. It was merely an observation about his less than enthusiastic greeting when my friends or dates came over to our house. He was, most often, lying on the couch, little, bald, head propped up on a pillow, winding down. Any announcement was greeted with the same monosyllabic response. I cannot spell it. It was just a mumble. It was kind of like *Aloha,* in that it could be translated to mean many things from *"nice to meet you"* to *"have a good time"* and all sentiments in between. I grew up with few face-to-face encounters with my dad. If he was angry with me, I was much too afraid to look at his face. If he was proud of me, he was much too uncomfortable to look at mine. And, I only remember one time hearing the words *I love you* in genuine tones. It was on the telephone, minutes after I woke up from major surgery. My mother had suddenly been taken in for emergency surgery while I was under anesthesia, myself. Dad had just found out that Mom was going to be okay and the call to me was in place of his physical presence at my sick bed. Otherwise, he would have been there with me. My parents always were. Anyway, he was so relieved about my mother's recovery that he just blurted it out: "I love you," he said. I was dumbfounded. I had longed to hear it my whole life, and now here it was, just when I least expected it. I said it right back, hung up the phone, and wept for hours. Yes, dads out there, it is *that* important. Yes, daughters out there, it hurts not to hear it. It is all right for you to be saddened by your loss. You are not the only child who craved a face-to-face fellowship with your daddy. You are not the only little girl who longed to hear loving words. It has been happening since the beginning of time. Even Emily, of Our Town fame, knew it. "Nobody ever really looks at each other," she said. That could be the war cry of every little girl who felt ignored by the one man who should have gloried in her presence—her dad. We suffer a kind of death when our fathers do not look us in the eyes and tell us they love us.

And, that is the real beauty of reconciliation. Once you have ceased all hostilities and taken steps to make things new, you can look in the eyes of a loved one and have sweet communion. There is nothing that can give you a quicker peek into the heart than a good, steady look in the eyes. It is a sure test. It cannot be pulled off if there are *any* bad feelings in the way. It will not ring true if complete honesty does not reside behind it. You cannot turn your head fast enough to hide your feelings from someone who knows you and looks into your eyes. This concept was never more emphasized than the last day I saw my goddaughter. As I carried her to her mother's van so she could go with her family to another state, I took great care not to look at her. The sadness was spilling out from my heart and swallowing was not going to work for too long. I forgot with whom I was dealing. Before I could place her in the car, she grabbed my face with her hands and looked right in my eyes. I knew she needed assurance that everything would be all right. I mustered every fiber of courage I had and smiled. Because our eyes met, she was comforted. As soon as she was gone, I fell apart. The eyes are, indeed, the windows of the soul and you cannot fool anyone who looks into them.

The Challenge of Standing Face-to-Face

Now, let's get back to the heartfelt desire of a daughter to have face-to-face communion with her dad. Perhaps, you can now understand why your father did not seek to commune with you. He knew that if he looked you right in the eyes, he would be discovered. The guilt would cause severe discomfort for some and regret upon regret for others. The very thing your tiny heart longed for was the thing your dad withheld in self-preservation. How could you have understood such a motive? You just thought there was something wrong with you. If the bad memories of your childhood are more like disappointments or un-met needs, I want you to try and forgive and forget. Maybe, your dad is at a stage wherein daily help or nursing is necessary. He is at his most vulnerable. Can you find peace and gentleness in your heart? Then look in his eyes whenever you can and tell him that you love him. It will only hurt for a while. And then, it will feel great. Eventually, you will feel it deeply too. Think about it.

Conversely, if your father was a perpetrator of lies and abuses, pray for him. That will be hard enough. You really have to *want* healing to manage that one. If this is impossible for you for whatever reason, then forget about him and let's get face-to-face with the Father of all. It is time, dear little sister, that you have sweet communion with your Heavenly Dad.

Communion That Heals

By now, you should know that our Father in Heaven truly cares about you and wants your fellowship. He is counting the hairs on your head, each of your breaths, and your very heartbeat. I think it is safe to assume that He *likes* you. And so, I hope we can agree that Father God *does* want to hang out with you. There are a few little items that may keep you from enjoying this kind of communion with the Creator of the universe. One problem, and probably the most restrictive, is your heart. Yes, I am talking about the very heart that God is even now monitoring beat by beat. That vital organ that keeps you going is, unfortunately, deceitfully wicked. Just like the three-year-old trying to get a snack between meals, we will cajole, lie, cheat, steal, pretend or any number of unflattering things to get "a cookie."

I believe that at this point in our relationship, you are ready to be face down in front of Father. I think you are finished trying to "make things work" yourself. I know you are tired and discouraged, because I have been there. So, let's just be authentic and humble. Most likely, when God found you, it was not under the best of circumstances. If that time is now, lift up your hand. He is there and He will take hold of you. It is our sovereign promise from The Lord. If there are still a few misgivings or questions in your head, be prayerful that God will make you teachable. Remember the words of the song, *Change My Heart*, and sing them, again. This does not make you weak. It proves that you are strong. I'll illustrate.

The *Glory* of the Glory of God

In my life, I have experienced lots of secular therapy in an attempt to gain control and peace. I'm not demeaning those times. Much good came from them. But, the story I want to tell has to do with those participants, usually men, who often commented to a support group something like: "I don't need therapy. That is for weak people," or one I *really* liked: "You people need this more than I do. I don't want to take up any of your time." Wow! We must have seemed really messed up! Anyway, my point is that it is really scary to tell others just how confused, helpless, sinful or discouraged we are. Often, we fear that if we give words to our thoughts or feelings, they may become the awful reality. That kind of fear can keep us frozen in trembling anticipation of the worst. Every step, word, or breath brings us a horrifying inch closer to being found out. The truth is that humbleness is for the strong and fearless, not for the weak and timid. Timid folks stay in the quiet darkness with their pain. You've got to be tough to get well.

And so, I am going to expect that you are ready and willing to meet Father on His terms because you know your need is great. I have good news and bad news. God has often come to meet with His kids on a personal level and that is surely good news. But, when He does visit, it is a little daunting. Perhaps you have heard of the Shekinah Glory of God. That is a terminology used to explain the overwhelming awesomeness of God's, physical presence. Moses got to see it, but only from the protective cleft in a big rock. Further, it was described as a bright cloud like a burning fire. The Israelites "saw" it as they wandered in the desert. By day, the Glory of God was a great cloud above the tabernacle and, by night, it was a pillar of fire reaching up to the heavens. When significant things were happening, the Glory of God was there. Still, when the Shekinah Glory rested over the tabernacle and the Mercy Seat, even Moses was not allowed to enter. Face-to-face with God is not possible in this mortal state. That is, sort of, the bad news.

How to Get to Know God

So how are we, little physical chunks of sugar and spice, supposed to commune with Father? First, you must know that He is there. You must believe His Word and trust in His promises. Once that is done, you have the rest of your life to get to know our Father by whatever means available. I know you know about the power of prayer. You've been calling out to The Lord since your early childhood. Of course, you know about the insights contained in God's Word for the beautification and sanctification of your life. And, as you read His Word, your eyes will be opened upon His "face."

But, I really want to get you off to a powerful start. I want you to experience rockets, bright lights, and brilliant flashes. You are about to embark on the ride of your life. Are you ready? Then open up to Psalm 46 and read verse 10. It simply says: *"Be still, and know that I am God."* And therein lies the single-most difficult thing for a wounded child to do—Be still. Remember, I know you. I know that silence is just an excuse to rewind and play old tapes, over and over again. I know that in-activity makes you fidget with pent-up nervousness. I know that before you go to sleep at night, all of your worries and problems loom large and frightful. And, I know that you understand that He is God and you are not. After all, if it is too quiet, might the scary things overtake you? If you quiet the screams of warning in your head, will your awful past happen all over again? Breathe deeply, sister, and go back to verse one. *"God is our refuge and strength, a very present help in times of trouble."* (Psalm 9:9, paraphrased) See? He is *present*. That means He is *here*. That means something significant is going to happen. That means He sees your face. Be still, and look into His. Rockets? Bright lights? Maybe not yet, but someday you will see. Tip your eyes toward Heaven and cry: "Abba!" Daddy is holding your face.

Chapter Three

Who Is to Blame?

And who is he who will harm you if you become followers of what is good? But even if you should suffer for righteousness' sake, you are blessed. And do not be afraid of their threats, nor be troubled.

1 Peter 3:13-14

As a teacher, I am often called upon to settle disputes among my students. If ever the blessing of Solomon's wisdom could come in handy, it would be at times like those. Mostly, I do not have the luxury of having observed the social holocaust. I am only included, hopefully, but not always prior to bloodshed. What transpires next is predictable and volatile. It usually goes something like this: Someone did something for no reason and someone else was just an innocent victim. Unh-huh. So, I have this bridge to sell you—. Commonly, I am able to get to the bottom of the story, but not before all participants speak at once and jostle for the superior position. As you may guess, usually all of the parties involved are guilty on some level. That's the blame game in a nutshell.

Sin is No Respecter of Persons

Nowadays, I call this phenomenon "sin spin." All of us know this verse: *"All sin and fall short of the glory of God."* (Romans 3:23) We just imagine that others do it and we don't. Placing blame has been with us since the beginning—literally. Certainly, we all remember Sister Eve and the soulful refrain about the serpent being at fault for her lapse of obedience. We've been at it ever since. My students blame each other. Brother blames brother. Sister blames sister. And, most of us, at some time or another, blame our parents. I'm not going to get clever here and make finger-pointing references. It's just too important for us to understand that *all sin and fall short.*

All means *all* and that means you and me. Now that we have the basics out of the way, I want to introduce you to my least favorite hymn. (Okay, maybe I shy away from singing *Refiner's Fire* the most. But, this one is a close second.)

It is with the utmost respect for Martin Luther that I confess I do not, necessarily, enjoy his hymn, "A Mighty Fortress." I love the lyrics. I love the man. I love the sweet and powerful sentiment. After all, the hymn comes from the Psalm quoted at the end of my last chapter. I mean, I *really* love the message. I just can't sing it. I yawn through the whole thing, I think, because it requires that muscle-tight, Shirley Temple chin-down, shoulders-back, belting timbre. Men sound awesome singing it. Women should just shut up and listen. Please, know that I mean no offense to my sisters who love to sing it. You just go ahead and sing out! But, please don't ask *me* to perform it. I don't have the energy. Still, I never want to miss some of the most powerful words ever penned and set to music. For valuable content this song rocks! And, it helps me to introduce our next subject and that is: Who is to blame for all of the evil that comes into our lives? Or, why do bad things happen that darken our lives for what seems like eternity? That was a real mouthful and I could spend chapter after chapter expounding on this concept. So, let's just cut to the chase.

Satan Comes to Kill, Steal, and Destroy

There is real evil in the world. We are sinners who love the darkness. It is only but for the grace of God that we are not all perverted beyond the wildest stretch of imagination. Someone out there revels in this fact. He is the enemy. He wants to kill, steal and destroy. He delights in your sorrow and celebrates your pain. He is the whisperer who instigates every wicked act ever perpetrated. He is Satan. He is real. He is powerful. He is also operating on borrowed time. That makes him mad and committed. He is after your peace. When you were robbed of it in your childhood, he was pleased. He is hate and deceit and cruelty, incarnate. Let's not kid each other. Blame whom you will, but know that Lucifer is the one who deserves your disdain, who has earned your disgust, and who will one day burn for hurting you. How's that for retribution?

By now you know that I will not accept a pity party for the powerless. I want you to get mad. I want you to get into the battle complete with helmet, sword, and shield. Most of all, I want you to stop making excuses and participating in sin spin. You are a daughter of the Most High God. It was for you that Jesus Christ took stripe after stripe on that awful day. How long will you allow *the one who will lose* the greatest battle in history to float your boat? As the hymn says, "the ancient foe seeks to do us woe." But, our Dad is bigger and stronger and smarter and *will* win in the end. As the hymn reminds us, "one little word shall fell him!" I choose the fear of the Lord, and I want that for you. This is a time for new beginnings, so I have something wonderful to share with you. There is power in the blood and, yes (as Carmen says), this blood's for you, true Believers in Christ.

When Judgment Comes

Just for a moment, let's take a step back. I don't want anyone thinking that I am going to accept the old excuse, "The devil made me do it." I'm not and you shouldn't either. When people do bad things or perpetrate harm against others, they need to be dealt with in the Biblical sense. I truly believe that Father God knows what needs to happen to cleanse sin. He has given us perfect advice in His book and does not need you or me to interpret it for Him. So, on that great judgment day, consequences *will* fit the crime and none will stand blameless on their own power. Therefore, it follows that any misery visited on your head because of a sinful and dishonorable father will be punished. If you were robbed of a peaceful childhood, that thought should be a little exonerating. I know it does not erase the scars. But, Jesus still has His and that serves as a reminder and a witness. Perhaps, your scars will do the same some day. Anyway, the fact that Satan is in the world and wreaking havoc upon us is not a good *excuse* for our disobedience and our failures. What I want you to understand from this is a real knowledge that the spiritual battle rages and you are in the way. That old liar will never become bored with his desire to harm you. He does not sleep or tire from his mission. And so, when he notices someone or something handy to use against you, he does it. My good news is that we have our own arsenal of protection. My bad news is that, often, we do not recognize the attack and, sometimes, it comes, seemingly, from out of nowhere when we least expect it. What is important is that we learn about our enemy so that we can defend and offend against him. Yes. You heard me. I want you to put on the full armor of God for protection. But, I also want you to spend some of your time messing up old Lucifer's party. We are called to stand in the gap and step out in faith. Those are action verbs and so let's look at the warning signs that Satan is afoot. Then you will know when you are under attack and can respond with strength.

Putting on the Full Armor of God

One of my favorite tactics to teach my students is the thorough study of an authentic example in order to spot a phony. In fact, those who are in the banking business are wise enough to expect their employees to know, with certainty, what authentic, legal tender looks like so that they can spot a counterfeit. I believe this technique will serve you well when the battle heats up. And so, I want to suggest that you remind yourself of the last time you were filled with God's spirit so much that you had a heaven-on-earth experience. For me, those times happen most often during prayer or worship.

When my daughter participated in a traveling, music ministry one summer, my husband and I went to retrieve her at the end of the tour. We were able to share a worship service with those kids who had been up close and personal with the Lord for three months, night and day. The music that filled that room was truly heavenly. I did not want it to end. I knew it was a foretaste of glory and it was awesome! I'm sure you have been there, too and so, that is what I want you to recall for a few moments. Try to remember what held your focus, the condition of your heart, the strength of your emotions, or the intensity of the feelings of fellowship. If your experience was anything like mine, you were transformed and transported "outside" of the world and yourself and all that was good enveloped your very being. Drink that in. Think about that experience a long time. I'm not going anywhere. Okay. Here is the news flash. That very feeling should be a daily goal. That's what we're shooting for in our walk and almost anything that gets in the way of that experience and that spiritual "high" is from the one who comes to kill, steal, and destroy. He hates your joy. He hates your communion. He hates your faith. And, he knows just what to do to short-circuit your commitment. Twenty-four seven, Satan is on the job.

The Way Satan Works

I hope that by now, you are angry or, even better, firmly resolved. If you are, you can begin to win the battle for your peace as we look at the devil's weapons of mass destruction. Sit up and take notice! You know what the "real thing" feels like. Now, we can compare it with the counterfeit. Of course, we cannot discuss in this one book every possible ploy perpetrated by "the destroyer." I just want you to be wary, be looking, and be protected. You will know when Satan is working because you know God's peace and can compare it with true evil. Still, I want to talk about some obvious traps and tricks. We have already talked about one of our enemy's favorite tactics-

--depression. But, just to round out that discussion, I have a story. I know you can hardly wait. (Ha!)

Before I was a Believer, I was married to my daughter's father. Were I an objective observer, both sides of the story could be told. But, I am not objective about those awful years. However, I am now informed about how it all happened and can share my experience with the hope of enlightening yours. As a result of childhood abuses, I experienced bargain-basement depression until the day I was saved. That defeated demeanor set me up to accept less than I deserved from relationships. Can you relate? If you can, you will have sympathy for the fact that I remained in abusive situations for intolerably long periods of time often telling myself that my lot in life was to be unloved and unlovable. The time I lost, overwhelmed with that kind of paralyzing sadness, was the tactic of none other than Satan. Do you know how I know that now? I know that because I have felt loved and lovable since that time. Father God has healed my sorrow and brought me peace and taught me that God does not want his children to be depressed. He wants us to have all that He has for us, because His very purpose in coming was to give us life and *that* more abundantly. And so, you must lock the door against depression. There. I said it. But, that simple sentence is one of the hardest tasks you will ever attempt. It is like one of the script cues for the TV show, "Bonanza." The cast members dreaded the simple sentence: *"The four Cartwright's mount up."* The sentence was only five words. Accomplishing the task often took hours.

Satan Uses Depression

I know how difficult it can be to lock the door against depression. I think I know you well enough to suggest that this is more easily done if you see depression as a weapon used by Satan to steal your peace. Get mad at him and kick him out of your life. The sadness will follow his sorry self back to hell. As he is retreating, tie on the belt of truth mentioned in the scripture and do not take it off again. You are loved. You are lovable. You are God's daughter. Therefore, depression is not for you. It is a counterfeit feeling—a lie from the pit of hell. Send it back there, because you no longer need a resting place in your heart and home for the devil. If you need to, sing verse three of A Mighty Fortress: *"And though this world with devils filled, should threaten to un-do us, we will not fear for God hath willed His truth to triumph through us."* That's cool. Our Father in Heaven is the real thing and you no longer need the phony.

So, now that you no longer struggle with depression, you can plan for smooth sailing, right? I wish I could promise that it will be so. Unfortunately, depression may try to re-visit you. The beauty of God's plan is in the knowledge that He will be there each time even when things look very dark or even impossible. The prophet Elijah counted so many victories in his life that you might think he was immune to depression. He was not. Even after great victories and miracles, fears and depression would take his peace. But, God was faithful. There was a plan. It is the same for you and that brings us to another weapon wielded against God's kids by the devil—Fear.

Satan Will Use Fear

I know that we have covered some of this territory, already. The point of this discussion is to help you recognize the source of these destructive feelings and defend against them. Fear cannot exist in the presence of a Holy God, at least, not the bad kind. As Believers, we choose the fear of the Lord because we know His power, His might, and His love for us. That is not the kind of fear that freezes us in our tracks. The kind of fear referenced here has a scientific or, at least, biological name in academia. It is called the "fight-or-flight response." It has universal characteristics, common to all of us: heart palpitations, sweating, a rush of adrenaline, tightening of muscles, etc. It is physiological and it feels awful! That is where the flight part comes into play. Running is the usual response. Freezing in place is a dumb response. I confess to more than one incidence of freezing. This terrible physical feeling keeps many of us from stepping into unfamiliar territory like witnessing, for example. It can keep little daughters from running from danger or impending threats. This fear can hold us hostage, cowering from the giants in the land or worse, envying them.

Though not 100% correct, Roosevelt was very wise when he said: *"The only thing we have to fear is fear itself."* As a grown woman, you can use this kind of logic. But, as a little girl, you were at the mercy of evil and the concept of logic was not in your vocabulary. That is why fear works so well for the devil. First of all, the world is a fearful place. Many bad things happen every day. To compound this, we are bombarded with messages that fear is a motivator, that it can be exciting, or that it is entertaining. Why do you suppose it is so universal to "hide" from a little baby and pop out and say "Boo?" The next time you play this "game" with a child, notice that he or she does not laugh or smile until they realize that the scare was harmless and they have survived. This kind of surprise is fun usually, but the underlying foundation for this kind of fun is fright. Who has not been surprised by someone sneaking up with the intent to startle him or her? Funny? Maybe. Scary? Sure. Evil? Probably not. Still, we learn a response to startling events and it is not always a pleasant experience. Then along comes falling, getting hurt, movies, news stories, and real-life events where Satan is a-foot. That leaves you pre-disposed to a fear response and to the degree that you feel impotent, you will struggle with survival.

I know that this will sound like bad news again, but just stick with me for the big finish. You see, Satan knows what you are afraid of and he delights in striking your Achilles heel whenever it is exposed. This is designed to steal your peace. I hope you are sufficiently angry because this is the good news: You are a child of the Creator of the whole universe. He is watching over you without fail. If you have proclaimed that Jesus Christ is your Lord and Savior, by the Biblical standard, Satan cannot take you. He is the impotent one. And, at the end of history, we will see just how sniveling and puny he is. I cannot wait! But realistically, we must deal with this attack of fear by putting on the shield of faith. It will protect you in all times of trouble. As a child of God, you will experience much of Father's faithfulness in your life. Please do not miss those times. Do not let those events fade from your heart and memory. Write them on your heart or write them (really) on a piece of paper and hang them on your bathroom mirror. Then, when you are afraid, call upon the Lord for peace. Invoke the name of Jesus. Ask your Father in Heaven for a hug and it will come. It did before and it will, again. That is a certain promise.

The Temptation of Sin

Now then, I hope you are feeling empowered by your Savior's promise. Unfortunately, this is no time to rest in the uncertain state of denial, believing that all is now well because you are at the ready. I do not mean to take the wind out of your sails, here. It is just that the devil has many tricks in his arsenal, and if he cannot trip you up by scaring you or making you sad, he will entice you to sin. That's a favorite of his because it hurts many more people than you. He can destroy entire families, churches, neighborhoods, countries or nations in one fell swoop. Nazi Germany is a great example of sin run amok. But, let's not leap that far. Let's just look at the sins you and I might fall into and, like the ripples in a pond, do the devil's work.

When was the last time you heard these words, *"I don't mean to be a gossip, but—?"* FYI: This is a signal to run, not walk, to the nearest exit. Gossip is an insidious cancer placed in our hearts and minds by Satan, only after he has convinced us that we are really "helping" by spreading it around. We then rationalize our behavior to others and ourselves, adding our own embellishments to the story, and "sharing it in love" to help a fallen sister or brother. You are foolish to believe this line of reasoning. God did not call you to "fix" everyone else's sins. He has called you to conform *yourself* to His image. Pray for your brothers and sisters, give advice from God's Word when asked or compelled, and keep those confidences as though they were yours. Otherwise, Satan will have a heyday in your home, your church, or your land.

Lest you believe that these circumstances and dangers only apply to gossip, get comfortable (or should I say uncomfortable) and consider this list of sins: Faithlessness, judgmental attitudes, conceit, selfishness, insensitivity, rudeness, lust, bitterness, cruelty, unforgiving attitudes, idolatry, greed, impatience, envy, pride, temper, unbelief, assumptive attitudes, disrespect, disobedience, negative or evil thoughts, and, hold on to your hat, anxiety. Oh, how I wish this was an exhaustive list. Sadly, there are plenty more sins where those came from. Little sins, you say. Everybody does it, you say. May I refer you to the comments on rationalization? No matter. I want you to place the blame for these onerous attitudes smack dab in the center of Satan's playground, because there is no place else he'd rather be. Now, I tell you this because I want you to recognize sin in your life before it rules your life. Even the mighty have fallen in the face of the devil's attack. Often, we get comfortable with our sin or become inoculated against its effect because we won't submit to an understanding of its importance. We are to be like Jesus. That is our requirement as an adopted child. It is the responsibility of our inheritance and not the blessing of grace. By the way, the father of your youth may not have known these things. He may not ever learn them but, even still, Satan will use that ignorance to extend his filthy cause.

Asking God to Strengthen You

I do *not* want you to think that I am excusing the behavior of your father by explaining the source of sin as masquerading in the person of the devil. We have a choice, you know. We can choose Jesus within the restrictions of our new nature. We can choose responsibility. God can change our hearts, and we can choose to do His Will based on that inward working of His Spirit. If, anywhere in your heart, there is a desire to do His Will, He put it there, and I say, go with it. Put on the shield of righteousness, lock it in place, and do not leave home without it. The temptations are all around and you will not be the only one hurt by giving in to them. You were hurt by your dad's choices. Your church was hurt by an uncommitted member's gossip. Your children or friends or mate will be hurt by your misdeeds, also. Take a moment to consider your personal sins. Be honest. Be brutal. Be as definitive as you would be with someone else, and then pray for forgiveness and the strength to change. There is something about working on your own problems and shortcomings that gives you patience and grace with others. I'm not nagging. I'm just reminding. That is good teaching. And, so is this:

> Finally, all of you be of one mind,
> having compassion for one another;
> love as brothers, be tenderhearted, be
> courteous; not returning evil for evil or
> reviling for reviling, but on the contrary
> blessing, knowing that you were called
> to this, that you may inherit a blessing.
> For He who would love life
> And see good days,
> Let him refrain his tongue from evil,
> And his lips from speaking deceit.
> Let him turn away from evil and do good;
> Let him seek peace and pursue it.
> For the eyes of the Lord are on the righteous,
> And His ears are open to their prayers;
> But the face of the Lord is against those who do evil. (1 Peter 3:8-12)

The Great Pretenders

I could not leave this subject matter without commentary on what I believe to be the greatest destroyer of our peace today. I consider it to be the most destructive because it is so hidden and sneaky. I come by this philosophy as a result of many hours of counseling with a never-ending stream of women on the verge of, and those swimming in, complete breakdowns. These dear sisters live lives of quiet desperation, on pins and needles, terrified that they will be found out or lose control of the situation. Often, they are the victims of a society that has grown to appreciate and respect individuality, success as defined in terms of income or career, and self-reliance as it illustrates personal power. They work full-time, shuttle the kids on a never-ending series of round trips, go to the gym, and help out at the church. They smile a lot. They joke a lot and they stifle screams of horror every day.

How about this one? Some of our little sisters jump headlong into ministries, giving it their all, settle for empty lives, dressed up with their many interests, and hide their paralyzing loneliness with smiles, jokes, and sincere concern for others. And then, they take it until they cannot take any more. Sometimes, there is an inciting event, like a husband who suddenly leaves after years of a wife's dedicated service, or a parent who dies, or a disappointment brought on by the failing of a pastor or leader. It does not really matter what starts the downward spiral. There are as many reasons as there are people. Whatever the reason, the fear is palpable and the look on their faces is heartbreaking. Their behavior borders on the psychotic and the illness is real, not imagined. These little sweethearts are heartsick, broken, and bleeding. Do not kid yourself into thinking that this kind of thing is an isolated event. I have spoken to three of them this week and it is only Sunday afternoon. They are frightened, confused, and feeling crazy. What brought them to this awful end? They do not know who they are. Their husbands or fathers do not know who they are. The pastor or teacher does not know who they are. Everyone has forgotten that there are rules when dealing with God's kids. These precious spirits have been disrespected, dishonored, over-loaded, abused, ignored, and unappreciated. They struggle to maintain the simple desire to live. They are your wives, sisters, neighbors, and yes, daughters. Given one gentle look or caring word, they will come apart at the seams. They are fragile and helpless. We have created them, and it is our duty to inform them of our sin. Sorry. It had to be said. Now, just what do I mean when I say we "created" these broken women? Let me tell you a story. No. Not really. (I'm joking.)

Being Part of the Solution

When my daughter was in the first grade, I was elected to be the PTA President at her elementary school. It was a daunting task for a twenty-five-year-old greenie. Nonetheless, I was determined to do the job well because it gave me more opportunities to be near my little angel. Remember, I was rabid about my motherhood. Anyway, one of the disappointing characteristics of leadership is that you are the target of much criticism that, by the way, can be a heinous sin. I was not immune to this attack. In fact, after every event or activity completed by our PTA, I received a call from the same woman complaining about my lack of leadership, or the lousy turnout, or any number of awful mistakes made while I sat at the helm. I tolerated the blasting with grace for about three months and then, I got wise. I looked for the name of my nemesis on the list of PTA members and (surprise), it was not there. I was ready for her next call. I asked: *"And, how long have you been a member of our PTA, Mrs. . . . ? Oh, really. Well then, when you become an active member of our organization, I would love to hear your opinion. Bye, bye!"* She never called again.

I know you are wondering how this relates to the fault we bear for the suffering of our sisters in the Lord, and you know I am going to tell you. If we are not actively engaged in the solution to the world's problems, we are part of the problem. That is the earth-shattering truth. Go ahead and be offended. Or, just consider the charges with your shoulders back and a strong desire to leave this planet a little better than it was when you arrived. The breakdown of the family is a real event. Fathers are leaving their responsibilities to their wives or, even worse, the government. Mothers are seeking careers outside the home without considering the kids. Christians are asleep at the wheel on such issues as godly marriage, godly relationships, godly education, godly government, commitment to fellowship, prayer, and the study of God's Word. We want big screen TV's and lots of cars. We want to eat out. We want lots of playtime. We want to be in charge of our own bodies even when another body grows within it. We don't want to be bothered by such irritating things as disciplining our kids or respecting our spouses. We want God around on Sunday and special holidays, but we do not want to clean the toilets at the church on Saturday. We are asleep in the light, apathetic to the truth, and running from our only source of true peace. You will never find joy or peace following the advice of the devil. You will reap what you sow. It is inescapable. God loves you too much to allow this kind of behavior to go un-noticed and unpunished.

> Wives, submit to your own husbands, as to
> the Lord. . . . Husbands, love your wives, just
> as Christ also loved the church and gave Himself
> for her. . . (Ephesians 5: 22, 25)

> Children, obey your parents in the Lord, for
> this is right. . . (Ephesians 6:1)

These words of God should be in your heart:

> You shall love the Lord your God with all
> your heart, with all your soul, and with all
> your strength. (Deuteronomy 6:5.)

> You shall teach them diligently to your
> children, and shall talk of them when you
> sit in your house, when you walk by the way,
> when you lie down, and when you rise up.
> You shall bind them as a sign on your hand
> and they shall be as frontlets between your
> eyes. You shall write them on the door-posts
> of you house and on your gates. (Deuteronomy 6:7-9)

Taking the Offense

When you have become an active member of God's family, I would love to hear your opinion. I'm not trying to be flippant. This is serious business.

Be a godly wife. Be a godly mother. Be a godly child. Be a god-fearing citizen. Parent, vote, and educate according to God's advice. Stop rationalizing why God is not at the center of every decision you make. That is counterproductive, and you are headed for a breakdown. Get thee to a fellowship and get help. You are worth it. Really.

This is the really interesting part. (I can say that without offending the author.) There are a few things you can do to foil Satan's plot. Together, we *can* keep him out of our lives, our marriages, our families, and our country. Heed these warning signs and take action as follows. . . .

There is No Victory in Fatigue

Do not allow yourself to be fatigued. If you are tired, you cannot fight the good fight. This is spiritual *war*, every bit as vicious as any war, perhaps more so because the stakes are so high. No one wants the guy at his back to be nodding off in the middle of battle. If you are tired, you will be no good to yourself or others. You will be irritable, think fuzzy thoughts, be impatient and jump to conclusions. Your memory will fail you. You will be more accident-prone. You will suffer more physical ailments: headaches, neck aches, back aches, etc. You will be the lousiest gift to your loved ones ever given. You will be even more useless than that wooden chicken your in-laws gave you for Christmas. When you are exhausted, the devil closes in for the kill. He whispers moans into your ears. He pokes at your body with aches and pains. He delights in your misery. How I hate him! So please, if you are not sleeping, find out why. Try anything safe and healthy to get some sleep. Quit working until midnight. The dishes will be there tomorrow. Put the kids in bed early. Take a warm bath. Light great-smelling candles and listen to really good music. Rest from the day's assaults. Finish each day with a word to Father. Request His protection and send Him your love. Satan hates that.

Seek Christian Fellowship

Next, surround yourself with people who love The Lord. You do not need friends among the Babylonians. You must invest in Christian relationships and flee from worldly relationships. Stay away from bars, and casinos, and pagan rituals. Do not tell me, after your life is in hell, that you thought you were strong enough to withstand the onslaught of the world. Peter was not. David was not. You are not, either. P.S. Your kids *really* are not. Think about it. If that is not compelling enough for you, I invite you to ponder the promise of our Father in Heaven that *"where two or three are gathered together in My Name, I am there in the midst of them."* (Matt. 18:20) The devil cannot be where God is. Gather. There is safety in numbers.

By now, we have become very good friends, I hope. You are realizing that I have common feelings and thoughts, and I am grateful that you are still reading. So, do not be afraid when I tell you I know what you are thinking. You are thinking that you have nothing to offer a group of Believers. You are thinking that good, godly people would not want to be with you if they knew your sinful heart. You are afraid of exposing too much of your need to others. If this is you, relax. A gathering of the saints is not akin to the Inquisition. They are as messed up as you are. Trust me. Our enemy uses isolation to keep you sad, depressed, and lonely. You can defeat him by reaching out to your brothers and sisters in the Lord. He is uncomfortable in that venue. He'll move on down the road to a more likely group of victims. By the way, you may just pick up a thing or two from this crowd that will serve you well in your personal walk with Jesus. That's what we call a bene!

Loving Yourself is Not Selfish

I am so excited to share this next point with you. This one you are going to like. I am inviting you to pamper yourself. You heard me right. I want you to do some nice things, just for you. This is not selfish. This is nurturing. Wounded daughters do not take care of themselves, ever. We give the biggest piece of meat at the evening meal to our husbands and sons. We give our dessert to someone else. We give up our place in line at the supermarket for an elderly person. We do not complain when the wait at the doctor's office is unusually lengthy. We are used to playing second (or third) fiddle. It is not that being concerned for others is a bad thing. That is not the point I am trying to drive home. I want you to appreciate that a lot of resentment can build up in the face of constant sacrifice. And so, you can chase away the devil by being kind to *you*. Still not convinced?

Imagine, if you will, searching the house for a birthday gift for your mother. Would you be satisfied to present a used bathrobe or half-empty bottle of cologne to the woman who gave you life? What if you wrapped it up in crumpled, used paper or just stuck it in a grocery bag? Could you do that? Would you? What an awful thought! Well, guess what? That is what you are doing every day of your life. You are letting the gift of yourself get trampled, used up, and crumpled, and then you are presenting it to your loved ones as their gift. What are you thinking? Do you not see that you are cheating your loved ones of the awesome gift that is you when you allow yourself to get drained of joy and peace? One day you will leave them to go to the Lord. Leave behind beauty and peace and loving memories of you. It will ease the sting of separation. That is in your heart, isn't it? I know.

Pray, Pray, Pray!

Finally, and certainly not conclusively, you need to commune with Father at every moment possible. When you are engaged in fervent prayer with God, Satan cannot harm you. When you are with Father, the devil runs in cowardly horror. But, that is not the only reason to pray. We pray to receive wisdom. We pray to receive peace. We pray to be heard. We pray in petition of our needs. We pray to bask in the beauty of God's throne room and catch a glimpse eternity. We pray to rest and re-charge. We pray to lift up our loved ones for blessings. We pray to be valued. We pray to be loved. We pray to change the world. We pray to change ourselves. We pray because Father tells us to. For the time spent with the Lord in prayer, you can be safe, whole, and home. Could it possibly get any better than that? I promise you that, if you spend plenty of quality time in the presence of Abba Father, your life will take on a new meaning and you will begin to wonder how you managed before. Time spent in prayer will just somehow fly by and you will find yourself wanting more of it. As you enjoy God's presence, Satan will flee and if he dares return, Father will protect you. You know, when life beats you up and you are sobbing with despair, most of us just want to talk to a friend or someone who understands us, without judging. Your Heavenly Father is the best of friends.

Satan Wants to Steal Your Joy

I hope you don't mind staying on the subject of God's love and genuine concern for you a while longer, because I want to share an insight with you. Of course, you have probably already realized the great lessons in these Biblical accounts. It takes a lot to get through to me, so please be patient while I explain. I know that a thorough understanding of the ploys of the devil will strengthen you in times of trouble and confusion and prepare you well to win on that battle ground. Remember, know your enemy and be victorious. I believe that one of God's goals, connected to these scriptural accounts, is to further arm us against the evil one. Let me explain.

The Temptation of Christ

The four gospels, with their unique perspective on the life, ministry, and death of Our Lord, contain accounts of a very curious event. I am speaking about the devil's attempt at tempting Jesus. The scripture tells us that, at the beginning of Jesus' ministry, he presented Himself before John the Baptist to submit to the foreordained sacrament of baptism. Pay careful attention to that word *submit*. It plays heavily in the proceedings. Do you recall that after being baptized, the heavens opened and the Spirit of God descended upon Christ as a dove? That was a time of joyful and sacred communion among the three persons of the Godhead. It was, indeed, a spiritual event of great magnitude. Jesus was affected by this sweet respite. Even though it pales by comparison, we often feel a minute taste of this after an awesome worship service or an intense time of intercessory prayer or at the conclusion of a blessing. It is not a coincidence that, at these types of moments, we are often set upon by Satan. The devil harbors a particular seething spite for useful persons. He would like to intercept your peace and frustrate your call. This is of special interest to those who may be beginning a ministry and feeling especially threatened. You most likely are a target for the old liar's wrath. Hang in there and follow the example of our Savior. These spiritual "triumphs" leave us tenderhearted, but also emboldened and strengthened for the test. Now, back to our review.

Jesus retired to the wilderness, fresh from the waters of baptism and spiritual communion, so that Satan might have a chance to do his worst. This is a powerful message to those of us who allow ourselves to be "cut from the herd", or who may forsake the fellowship of the saints in times of great need. I already warned you about being alone in your suffering. That is target time, and you must avoid it. The devil will not miss the opportunity to get you alone. Jesus, of certainty, was equal to the task. In conquering the trial, the Lord would also prove Himself to be greatly victorious and exalted in His own strength. It was, all at once, His perfect opportunity to show godly humility and, all the while, confusing and confounding Satan in the bargain. Additionally, it was His intent to comfort His sheep in the knowledge of God's unparalleled power to deliver His children. As we watch the unfolding of events, three goals of the devil are clearly illustrated. He will attack us by the lusts of our flesh, our desire for unholy power, and the Achilles heel of our ego. Ultimately, Satan's goal is to overthrow your relationship with God, as your Father. (What have I been saying?) He tried these very tactics with Jesus. Go ahead and laugh in disdain. It *is* ridiculous. Now, compose yourself and let us study the content of the text.

Many believe that the devil may have come to Jesus as an angel of light. That's funny too, because it is hard to imagine that Satan did not know he could not fool God. At any rate, in times of wrenching temptation, be wary of those who seem too good to be true. (Repeat the, if-it-looks-like-a-duck chant in your head.) First, Satan suggested that Christ change stones to bread, knowing of His continuous fasting. He had hoped to get Jesus to question the voice of truth from God, cause Him to distrust His Father, and be His own power, while gratifying his own hateful desire to get Jesus to do his cowardly bidding. And, herein lies one of the greatest examples of masterful warfare. Jesus answered with scripture. Didn't I tell you that the Word is *the* sword of truth, our best weapon of offense? The Lord knew it and He used it. He said: *"It is written, 'Man shall not live by bread alone, but by every word that proceeds from the mouth of God.'"* (Matt. 4:4) He is telling you to stay in the Word. The devil was certainly confounded. But, you know, my dear sister, that the devil is a restless and unwearied adversary. He will continue to attack your flesh, again and again. Our Savior knew this and provided this example. Father will provide. Do not forget that it is better to live poorly on the fruits of God's goodness, than to live plentifully on the proceeds of our own efforts of sin. In times of despair, read again the words of our Father and be comforted. He will care for you.

Now, the chronology of the next two temptations is reversed in Matthew and Mark. This should not be of great concern. It is not uncommon for two accounts to report things from varying perspectives. The most important fact is that the content is the same. So, let's just agree to discuss Satan's suggestion that the Lord throw Himself off the pinnacle of the temple. Why the temple, you ask? Well, sister, the temple was revered, and it was large and easily seen from a great distance. The devil specializes in trying to make a laughing stock of God. He does that when he hurts you. But, Jesus was so-o-o God. When Satan suggested that this act would bring the Savior admiration and acceptance, guess how our Lord answered him? Yep. You've got it. Jesus repeated the scripture: *"It is written again, 'You shall not tempt the Lord your God.'"* (Matt. 4:7) That sounds like a serious warning, and I would be listenin', mister! Again, Jesus shows submission in the test and reminds God's children of the ministering of angels promised by Father. He does *not* over-step God's promises. Foiled again. By the way, did you notice that the puny, old devil had to suggest that the Lord cast *Himself* down? He did and does not have the power to *make* God *do anything*. Never has. Never will. What Satan will do is try to attack you with your own ego, accordingly. Do not be his yes woman. He does not value you in the least and delights in your misery. Hate him, responsibly.

Finally, the devil takes Jesus to the highest of mountains so that He may survey the whole world in its awesome expanse. The devil shows worldly temptations as charming and to be desired. He appeals to Jesus' pride of life and tries to get Him to believe that God has abandoned Him. Ever been there? It is a wicked and cowardly trick---the promise of power he cannot grant. He is like a vile and immoral politician who makes promises he cannot, nor ever intended to keep. Worship me, he pleads, and I will give you the whole world. This time he went too far. Jesus rebukes: *"Away with you, Satan! For it is written, 'You shall worship the Lord your God, and Him only you shall serve.'"* (Matt. 4:10) I think this line was delivered with extreme emphasis. Our Lord was disgusted, upon which Satan made a shameful and inglorious retreat.

Jesus, Our Greatest Example of Strength

At this point, angels come to minister. We are encouraged by the Savior's willingness to suffer this time of temptation to show us the power of obedience and remind us to trust Father. Our Redeemer stood His ground for Himself and for us. The devil emptied his arsenal to no avail, so he turned tail and ran. But, I don't want you to miss this little tidbit. Satan, even in this cowardly retreat, lies in wait to attack at a weaker moment. He has learned nothing. He is truly overcome with evil will. What can we learn from this? The devil has nothing to offer you. You have nothing to gain and everything to lose if you succumb to his old, tired, dumb tricks. Now, you know what they are. Watch always and be ready with the full armor, right? Right.

Let's review then. The evil enemy who robbed you of your childhood was Satan. He is not finished harming you. It is of utmost importance that you no longer deliver yourself up to him in a little box. He will attack you on very familiar territory. He specializes in the lusts of the flesh, the worship of the self or ego, and the deification of your personal will. He was at work in the lives of your parents. He was at work in your relationship with your father. He is at work today in your wounded soul. You know what to do. Lock him out. Put on the belt of truth, the helmet of salvation, the breastplate of righteousness. Pick up the sword of His Word, the shield of faith, and the sandals of the gospel of peace. In all things persevere and entreat God to be with you. Now, get out there and win one for the Lord!

Chapter Four

What Do We Do Now?

*But you are a chosen generation,
a royal priesthood, a holy nation, His
own special people that you may proclaim
the praises of Him who called you out of
darkness into His marvelous light; who
once were not a people but are now the
people of God, who had not obtained
mercy but now have obtained mercy.*

1 Peter 2:9-10

A New Creation

So, HERE we are. We have come to the place in our journey where we must face our last challenge. This is the time for our final answer. Now, we must reflect on our reflection. We have come to this place together to make good the complete healing that is yours. If you are not reeling from the many things we have learned about our Heavenly Father, start over. You missed a few things. But, I think I can assume that you have at least begun to appreciate who you are and what that means for your future. You are no longer bound by the sins of your earthly father. You are not a prisoner of your past mistakes. You do not believe that you are dispensable. And so, it is time to return to the face in the mirror and record the changes observed. This is our most important exercise because it will determine if our time together has been well spent. If you have come to this point as a Believer in the sovereign God of our universe who has revealed Himself, in-errantly, in the Biblical scripture, you already trust in Father's promise that He has made a new creation out of you. He has given you a new heart and is using this book to sanctify your walk. Look into the mirror and experience the next few pages as a personal sermon intended to bring healing and peace. However, if you are still searching for a sure knowledge of your relationship to the Creator, please consider the next few pages as a witness of truth intended to draw you closer to His Will. I believe that, if you are God's child, He will open your heart and you will be made whole in Him. The scripture tells us:

> Therefore, if anyone is in Christ, he is a new creation; old things have passed away; behold, all things have become new. (2 Corinthians 5:17)

Your Heart Can Change

Now then, you have the chance for a fresh start. It is truly the best of all of God's gifts and the very reason I am able to share my thoughts with you. Before the Lord changed my heart, I would not have cared so much about you. I was busy caring about me and running around a self-imposed hamster wheel of sin. I was going nowhere as fast as I could. But, if you remember when I began this journey with you, I confessed to being hijacked into this ministry. God would not let me rest until I brought this message to you. This is pay-off time, and so I am not kidding. I want you to look *into* the mirror as I share these words. Our Father in Heaven is Holy, Holy, Holy, and has much to tell you now. So, look carefully and listen intently. Hear His voice:

Your Message From God

How I love you, my precious little one. You are my friend and my blessed servant whom I have chosen. I remember when you were forming inside your earthly mother. I rejoiced in each new milestone, caused your eyes to form, your heart to beat, and your hair to grow. My heart is filled to over-flowing with you. I remember your tiny fingernails on the day you were born into my world. I can even still hear your weak cry, fresh from the safety of your mommy's body. You are a glorious and wonderful child! Do not be dismayed in times of need. I was there when you rode your first two-wheeled bike and with anticipation, I guarded you from serious harm. I made your skin to glow in its unique way. The twinkle in your eye was placed there by Me. When you cried out in anguish, I did not turn away. I was by your side through it all. I have never left that place. The pain that you have suffered did not go unnoticed and will not go unpunished. For I, the Lord will not be mocked. My precious daughter, I will seek retribution. On the day that you saw your first flower, I sent the breeze that cooled you, even as My Hands smoothed your hair from your eyes. I am keeping your first A+ in my memory. If I close my eyes, I can hear your voice singing, *"Jesus loves me, this I know."* It is sweet incense to my being. Each time you lift up your prayers of gratitude and supplication, I am listening with love and compassion. I am with you always. I will hold you up daily by my righteous hand and defend you from all who come against you. I am the Lord, your God. It was with great pride that I stood by you when your courage came through as truth. I had seen the sin, but marveled that you were obedient to My Law. Each time you obey My Will, I am filled with joy. I am in the peaceful whisper of the Holy Spirit in your times of decision and confusion. It is my desire to bless you in abundance as you step out in faith. I wish to give you supernatural gifts as you bless others in My Name. How gratified I was at your kind act toward a frightened neighbor on that night calamity visited. *You* are My work and My glory. I am holding the lamp at your feet as you maneuver through the treacheries of life. I have predestined you to be My Child and I *will not* let you go! Please call home soon. Love, Father.

Changed by Perfect Love

Are you looking in the mirror? I hope that you are and that you see what I know is there. If you are still not convinced that our God places great value in your life, look in the mirror again and read that last paragraph, out loud. Hang those words on your mirror and read them, daily. Record it into your cassette player and "play it again, Sam!" Do not move another step until the message has stamped itself inside you, on the cellular level. God, the perfect Father, loves you. He *loves* you. He *loves* you. He *loves* you. HE LOVES YOU!

That ought to hold you.

There is one more thing we must do before I let you go. It is not an easy concept to accept because our lives have sometimes required us to do just the opposite from what I will suggest. In the utter despair to protect ourselves, we build fortresses of such strength that the re-model can be extensive. Think of this as an episode of *Trading Spaces*. Father God wants to re-decorate your life for a new beginning. (Don't worry. He is not like Hildy! P.S. Have you noticed that *her* home is beautiful? What's up with that?)

Called to Forgive

As my final gift to you, I want you to experience the sweet feeling of forgiveness. First, I wish for you to extend it to others. I pray that, in this time we have spent together, you have realized that each of us is a sinner of the most extreme, in dire need of a Savior. Last, but most assuredly not least, I want you to forgive yourself. It is time to be about Father's business. And so, I am going to tell you a story.

Growing up in a large family affords many blessings. That is nice. I do not have to tell you that the opposite can be true. Growing up in a large family may also create little glimpses into the halls of hell. If you are from a large family, right now you are either rolling your eyes or nodding, emphatically. Anyone who has had to share a bedroom or one bathroom with someone of the opposite ilk can testify to the horror. You see, my little sister was a clean freak. I was not. Okay. The family joke was that I had three colors of sheets: white, gray and black. Yes. They were the same sheets. Ha. Ha. But, I digress. The fact that I had to share my bedroom with *"Martha Stewart"* was grounds for constant battle. Once, the little darling even a-fixed a tapeline down the center of the room to delineate between "Beauty and The Beast" with the express instructions that I could not cross the de-militarized zone. Now, lest you think that our bedroom was the only hotspot in the house consider that I had three sisters and three brothers. We all shared bedrooms and bathrooms. These conditions often erupted into civil wars. We can laugh at this now. In fact, it is a source of hilarity at family gatherings. Still, my brothers and sisters and I spent many wasted hours filled with anger and thoughts of revenge over what seems today were insignificant issues. My mother, God bless her, did her best to keep the screaming, tantruming, and bloodshed to a minimum. She was mostly successful. What stands out in my mind now is that I have forgotten every, single thing that we ever fought over in those formative days. I know that I felt strongly, at the time. But, I cannot help but wonder where the anger went. Actually, I am getting ahead of myself, here, because these past skirmishes are not the conclusion of the story. The real sorrow happened much later. Just don't forget that we had established a pattern of harboring ill will early on.

On the morning of my wedding to my wonderful husband, my father suffered the stroke that left him profoundly disabled for the rest of his life. He did not walk me down the aisle. I will always regret that. The important content of this experience was in what happened after this family-changing event. For six months after daddy's stroke, my mother and sisters and I, with occasional help from my brothers, cared for dad at home. This is another reason why I understand the stages of grief. We were all over that baby. Anyway, my mother was a willing martyr from way back. (I am not being demeaning here. She chose it because she valued un-selfishness above herself.) Because of the high demands of dad's constant care, my mother suffered a fatal heart attack in January of 1996. It was also a fatal blow to our family dynamic. My eldest sister chimed the death knell the night of mama's death when she said: *"We have lost the heart of our family."* That proved to be prophetic. What followed, after that, was a gradual decline of family fellowship and, finally, the demise of any sense of its importance. Holidays, which had been paramount for family time, began to be honored apart. Birthdays went un-celebrated. The information system between us broke down, completely. Babies were born, family members were hospitalized, and new houses were purchased without any shared sense of camaraderie. It was a great time for the devil. Resentments built up to explosive proportions and rationalizations were rampant. The blame game was alive and well. But, it had not reached its zenith. The final harbinger of the death of my family was in the adjudication of the family fortune. During better times, my parents had set up a family trust to be distributed at the proper time by my brothers. The gory details are not necessary. Just months before, and upon the death of my father, the lawsuits and threats abounded. Comments like: *"I will never forgive him or her for this"* were common. It was hell on earth, and the loneliness was palpable. I missed my mother. I missed my father. And, I missed my *family*.

God's Mercy Heals Us All

And then, we were mercifully blessed by the grace of God. My sisters and I reached out to each other to un-tangle the mess. It is true that nothing unites better than a common enemy. What we understood to be injustice was the common enemy that "glued" us together. My brothers stood firm in their resentments. Even at my father's funeral, two brothers continued the rivalry and refused to ride in the limousine to the cemetery. I had to chase one of them around the cemetery to tell him I loved him. He, to this day, has not forgiven or forgotten. I miss him. But, I am speaking about grace, here. To my great joy and, I know, the approval of my Father in Heaven, my sisters and I have begun, again. I believe that, at this winding down time in our lives, the love between us will grow sweeter and stronger each day. I stand in awe of a God who can heal this kind of brokenness. Thank-you, Jesus.

What happened to cause the forgiveness among my siblings to begin to flow? Each of us had to clarify for ourselves what was truly important. We needed a common focus. Satan had interrupted our lives, and we had to take them back. We had lost so much when our mother and father left us. We could not afford to lose it all. God brought us to the depths of despair only to rescue us, again.

Plugging to God's Power

It is true for you now. How long will you live with anger and resentment in your heart? Is it bringing you the peace you crave, or is it destroying all that you hold dear? Do you begin each new day with anticipation for the blessings and gifts awaiting you, or is there a darkening dread at the foot of your bed? (I did not intend to wax poetic. But, it's cool, huh?) I know that you get my point. The sadness and destructive oppression that plagues us when we experience negative emotions leaves us hollow, exhausted, and discouraged. We cannot find a reason to hope for a better outcome. We are just too tired and have lost any desire to reach for joy.

I think of this the way I think about my vacuum cleaner. (Stick with me. I have not lost all reason.) I have been a housewife long enough to have wrestled with more than one appliance. There have been days that the smallest portion of my day was spent in actual cleaning or home-making activities because the greatest portion of my time was spent repairing, rigging, or praying to an appliance, longing for just one more successfully completed chore. Are you with me? At any rate, I *do* know a few little survival tricks with vacuums, toilets, faucets, and door hinges. I know that if my vacuum will not pick up the yucky stuff, there is a trouble-shooting hierarchy. I goes something like this: Run the machine over several more chunks of debris to make sure you did not imagine a problem, re-plug the cord, (the alternative response could be to try the top *and* the bottom wall receptacle) reel all strings off of the beater bar, jam a straightened hanger down the hoses, replace the belt, and finally, check to see if the collection bag is full. Don't you make fun of me. You do it too, and I have a point here. You see, if the mechanisms are clogged, in any way, the vacuum ceases to accomplish the task for which it was created. Whew! That was a long way to a simple truth.

When you fill your life with the crippling emotions of revenge, unforgiveness, harsh judgments, and hatred, you become clogged and unable to accomplish the task for which you were created. It is time to empty the useless garbage from your life and replace it with goals, rich with integrity. You must forgive yourself for the mistakes of the past and forgive those who have trespassed against you and get on with it. And remember, you may never return to the "dumping ground" of the past and retrieve old business. When you move past old experiences, all information connected to the sin should self-destruct like those nifty messages in *Mission Impossible*. The scripture says it like this:

> For as the heavens are high above the earth,
> So great is His mercy toward those who fear Him;
> As far as the east is from the west,
> So far He removed our transgressions from us. (Psalm 103:11-12)

Today, when I am dealing with forgiveness, I visualize a scenario one of my students created. This particular little fellow was fascinated by the volcano. There could not possibly be a lesson on the volcano that was too long or too involved. One day, he said to me, "Miss Joyce, what if you fell into a volcano? Oh, I know. You wouldn't even hit the hot lava before you would burn up, entirely. You might not even fall two feet before you were toast!" I think of this whenever I am working to forgive myself or someone else for a disappointing event. I try to toss the experience into hot lava and turn it into instant toast. That's how true forgiveness works. We forgive, and then we forget. We are to forget so thoroughly that we never regurgitate the offense, again. As the *Deep Thoughts* author once said, *"If you lose your keys in hot lava, let them go, man, because they are gone."*

All kidding aside, a fresh start is only a victory if the "old things pass away", as the song says. Given enough time, most scars fade to an imperceptible shadow. Given enough understanding of the forgiveness extended to us by Our Savior, harsh feelings toward ourselves or another person vanish in the volcano of grace. As I contemplate another holiday season without my father and mother, I am overwhelmed by a burning desire to gather my loved ones around me, while I can. I do not have time for grudges. I do not have time for retribution. I crave the peace of reconciliation, and I pray for the strength to obtain it. This I desire for you. And this, I know will bring the healing that you have ached for your whole life. God will give you the help that you need to learn this important concept. Pray for His blessing as you step into the new light of your fresh start. Take a deep breath (really big) and release, release, release.

The Purpose in Your Life

It is with regret that I share a final word with you. As I write these words, I truly feel a kinship and fellowship with each soul whose life may be affected by my offering. Call me crazy, but I feel like I know you and that you are my friend. I believe that it would not be honoring to the calling of my Father to leave you without a suggestion for filling up the "holes" left in your life from this intimate housecleaning. Abba Father knew we would need a worthy task to complete our lives and so He gave us a perfect example of the purpose-driven life in the person of Jesus Christ. Of all who have lived, Jesus is the only one worthy to exact justice from His tormentors. He was the perfect sacrifice, un-spoiled by sin of any kind. He did not deserve punishment. And yet, Jesus during His last hours showed us, His children a model of perfect service. Yes, I said service. The God of us all used His last moments in this mortal state to kneel and wash the feet of His disciples. He lifted the bar for us and shared the power and beauty contained in the heart of a servant. That is what you must do, now. You must cultivate a servant's heart. This is why you are here. You know who you are now. The final step is to serve the purpose you were created to serve. I promise that of all of the concepts we have discussed this is, perhaps, the most vital to perform. If you really seek the peace that surpasses all understanding, get on your knees and wash a few tootsies. Jesus said: *"The first shall be last and the last shall be first."* (Matt. 20:16) This is not about who goes to the front of the lunch line. This is about honoring Jesus' sacrifice and "picking up your cross and following Him." It is not a suggestion. It is a commandment. If you are still not convinced, I have to tell another story. This is your fault.

A True Servant's Heart

I once knew a mother of extraordinary character. She was the epitome of graciousness and industry. Her home was not fancy or exceptional in any way. In fact, this family lived in a fixer-upper and when I say lived, I mean *major living*. There were thirteen children in the family, a farming father, and this amazing mom. She was not what the world would consider beautiful or successful. She wore heavy glasses, rimmed with black plastic frames, had prematurely graying hair, and fought the battle of hip expansion like most of us. When I first met her, my family had just descended on their home without any notice, whatsoever. They were preparing to have their evening meal, and so I intended to simply pay respects and be on our way. I did not know with whom I was dealing. Before I had time to gather my tiny family in an apologetic farewell, super mom was setting three more place settings at her family supper table. At first, I was embarrassed, feeling like a real inconvenience. And then, I watched her. Cupboards opened to unveil dozens of jars of home-canned foods. Additional jars were opened and prepared before I could even seat my family. Talk about fast food! This little farm mother was the most gentle and unselfish hostess I have ever known. By the way, her thirteen children all had a part in the preparation of the meal, scooping up little brothers and sisters, setting out plates and cups, opening jars, and serving the food. Today, we would think that we had fallen into an episode of *Little House on The Prairie*.

This account I share to get to the real illustration. Many months later, this little family was visited by tragedy. Their little farmhouse was suddenly engulfed in flames from some bad wiring. This incredible mother had just had surgery on both of her feet and was confined to bed for convalescence.

When the fire broke out, her two smallest children were napping in the room where the fire started. Immediately upon leaving her sick bed, this blessed mom hobbled throughout the house, chasing her children to the safety of the front yard. Because the upper floor, where the trapped children lay, was largely involved in the fire, she grabbed a ladder from the garage, propped it against the window to the bedroom where her babies lay asleep, and climbed, with bleeding feet, to their rescue.

Before the fire department could arrive, she pulled both of those kids to safety, limped to the front lawn, counted her precious children to assure herself that all were safe, and because of the excess stress of her heroism on her heart sunk to the grass and went home to be with the Lord.

I cannot think of this little family without feeling ashamed of my own pitiful life complaints. But for you and I right now, I want this godly mother to stand as an example of putting our priorities in the right place. I want her life and death to be a goalpost for the rest of us as we try to understand what Father's calling on our life may be. I can think of no other real-life experience that better illustrates a servant's heart.

In the end, our Father in Heaven expects us to perform similar acts of heroism and service to His glory. It is all that really counts and it is all that really heals brokenness. To have a ministry in this life is the greatest gift. To be a mother or wife or sister or friend is our most cherished source of joy. It is given us by God, and it is the surest step to becoming like Jesus that has been offered. Paul said it best:

> Yet indeed I also count all things loss
> for the excellence of the knowledge of
> Christ Jesus my Lord, for whom I have
> Suffered the loss of all things, and count
> them as rubbish, that I may gain Christ
> and be found in Him. . . (Philippians 3:8)

Called to Serve

And you see, sweet sister, the healing that comes from forgetting our own sorrows and pain is un-mistakable in its power. Our Father and Jesus know this truth. I am reminded of the story I heard on Christian radio, years ago. A young man was walking the streets of a third-world country and was over-whelmed by the large numbers of suffering people. He was especially touched by the children, starving and shoeless, reaching out their tiny hands for comfort. In his torment, he cried out to the Lord, *"Why, Father, why? Can You not help these suffering children? Will You not send help?"* He was surprised and humbled by the soft answer, coming from the whispering spirit, *"I did send someone. I sent you."*

Please look around yourself as we spend these last moments together. The Lord of Hosts has a job for you to do, and you have tarried long enough. Take the sweet words of this hymn with you: *"Take my life and let it be, consecrated Lord to Thee. Take my hands and let them move, at the impulse of Thy love."* And, only then will you be able to lay your crown at the feet of Jesus. Make haste. You do not know how much time you have left.

I believe it will be helpful, at this time, to remember an account in the tenth chapter of Mark. Here we find recorded the request of James and John, the sons of Zebedee, to be *seated* on the right and left hand of Jesus in glory. How naïve they were! We know from the rest of the account that the disciples did not fully realize what was to happen, so very soon, to our Savior. They must have been laboring under the false belief that this Jesus would be a ruler in the land and that they would be honored among men for their position. Nothing could have been further from the truth. In fact, when the test came, many of them denied even knowing Him for the purpose of self-preservation. Jesus quickly informs the two that this honor is not His to give: *"It is for those for whom it is prepared."* Mark 10:40b.

And then, Jesus issues a kind of warning as He explains that those who think to exercise authority over others will be surprised at their (eternally) lowly position. Jesus concludes:

> But whoever desires to become great among you shall be your servant. And whoever of you desires to be first shall be slave of all. For even the Son of Man did not come to be served, but to serve, and to give His life a ransom for many. (Mark 10: 43b-45)

We are here for a great purpose and much of that purpose has absolutely nothing to do with us. Do you feel small? It is okay to feel small sometimes because that feeling can grow a new perspective in the heart of God's children. Those who do not belong to God are angered by this concept. Those who acknowledge and understand the sacrifice of the Lord are humbled by it. Which one are you?

As You Serve, Keep Your Focus on God

Maybe I know what you are thinking, right now. There is an important truth to understand here that may only be questioned by wounded little girls who are all grown up. People with other issues might not even catch this. But, I think I know you and so I proceed. Being a servant often has a dark underbelly. Those of us with self-worth issues often assume that martyrdom is a kind of service. We commit all of our energy in serving others and deny the facts surrounding it. This is a good time to remember the account of Martha and Mary, two sisters with the joyful appointment of entertaining the Savior in their home. Mary is said to have stayed at the feet of Jesus to hear His every word. Martha, however, was busily engaged in preparing the most elaborate feast within her capability. She was resentful of a sister who did not seem to ascertain the need to help with the meal preparation. She even called upon Christ to intervene and set Mary straight. Oh-oh.

> And Jesus answered and said to her, 'Martha, Martha, you are worried and troubled about many things. But, one thing is needed, and Mary has chosen that good part, which will not be taken away from her.' (Luke 10:41-42)

Go ahead. Let out a little yelp. It used to anger me, also. You see, I am a Martha. If the table decorations for the fellowship dinner do not match *exactly*, I am a mess. I can often be seen running to the store at the last minute if there are not enough rolls for the casserole. (P.S.: I probably don't need to tell you how often I have left-over food due to my freaking out.) Nonetheless, Martha's desire to be a servant was not the problem. The problem lay in her need to impress Jesus with her elaborate gift and her self-deprecating presentation. Jesus was gentle, but not impressed. Should Mary have helped in serving the group? Sure. But, serving the group needed to be a simple offering stimulated by the *sharing* of a meal. I mean, *Jesus was there!* Often, we miss the Spirit while we prepare the lesser sacrifice. Be Martha but be at the foot of the cross and God will provide the meal.

To Be Like Jonathan

If these words have not convinced you of the worth of cultivating a servant's heart, then I will just have to get tough again. I wish to refer you to the relationship between Jonathan, the son of King Saul, and David, the giant-killer. If you recall, upon the slaying of the giant, Goliath, by the boy, David, a mortal kinship developed between Jonathan and David that is un-paralleled in scripture or anywhere else that I can recall. So much had happened leading up to this friendship. The ark had been taken by the Philistines and returned at the culmination of some really bad luck visited on the miscreants. David, a young man, had slain the giant with a stone and the giant's own sword, and Jonathan had sown some renegade oats in a few skirmishes of his own. I think that the two boys were probably like so many teenagers whose youthful friendships last a lifetime and shape the future. However, it is in the eighteenth chapter of 1st Samuel that we see the true level of commitment and the condition of Jonathan's heart.

> Now when he had finished speaking to Saul, the soul of Jonathan was knit to the soul of David, and Jonathan loved him as his own soul. (1 Samuel 18:1)

Did you hear that? *The soul of Jonathan was knit to the soul of David.* If that does not tell the story of their friendship, continue reading the account.

> Then Jonathan and David made a covenant, because he loved him as his own soul. And Jonathan took off the robe that was on him and gave it to David, with his armor, even to his sword and his bow and his belt. (1 Samuel 18:3-4)

Death to Self

Everyone knew what this meant. Jonathan had recognized the will of God in the future of David. Jonathan understood that Father had chosen his friend to rule, apart from the customary inheritance. And, in every subsequent battle or challenge, Jonathan remained true to his covenant and loyal to his friend. He was a man of great integrity and a friend, indeed. But, please don't miss some important concepts, here. First, understand that the two friends made a *covenant*. This is almost foreign to those of us who live in an age where even a signed contract often means nothing. To the dismay of our Father in Heaven, even Christian brothers and sisters live faithless lives without integrity daily. That is very sad, but it is certainly not the way

Jonathan and David saw it. Most especially for Jonathan, this covenant meant everything to him. He gave up his throne and, eventually, his life in the service of his friend and his God. Even as the scripture states, *"he loved him as his own soul."* This was the heart of a true servant. This was the power of a committed life. This was the picture of a friend. This reminds us of the greatest servant of all—our friend, Jesus. And, this brings us to what could be considered the life's verse of every servant heart, in the words of our truest Friend:

> These things I have spoken to you, that My joy may remain in you, and that your joy may be full. This is My commandment , that you love one another as I have loved you. Greater love has no one than this, than to lay down one's life for his friends. (John 15: 11-13)

If you desire the joy of the Lord to remain in you, lay down your life, battered and bruised though it may be, and pick up the cross and follow Jesus. Feed the hungry, clothe the naked, and give living water to the thirsty. You will overcome the world. You will triumph over your past. And, you will become the child of God that you were made to be. Remember:

> Inasmuch as you did it to one
> of the least of these My
> Brethren, you did it to Me. (Matt. 25:40b)

Pray the prayer, *"Make me a servant."* Your days of darkness are over. P.S. I love you.

> But now, O Lord,
> You are our Father;
> We are the clay, and You our potter;
> And all we are the work of Your hand. (Isaiah 64:8)

Invitation to Salvation

I would be remiss if I did not take a few final moments to extend a vital invitation to my new friends. Whether you have enjoyed this book as a study to enhance your ministry, as a journey toward a deeper commitment to Christ, or to seek healing from a lifetime of pain, the next few sentences may be the most important of your life. Many of you have come from strong, Christian backgrounds and have little need to re-visit your past. Still, the Bible tells us that all sin and fall short of God's glory. That means that each of us is in dire need of a Savior. If you have come to a decision point in your life and are seeking the peace that passes all understanding, Jesus is waiting to bless you.

If you are not a Christian, you need to know that Father God is Holy, Holy, Holy and that sin cannot co-exist with Him in eternity. Jesus Christ is the sinless sacrifice who came to seek and save the lost. He lived the life we could not live, died for all of the sins of His children, and rose again on the third day to secure eternity for us. If your heart is reaching out for a Savior now, then God is drawing you. Simply pray with a humble heart that God will forgive your sins, that Jesus will come into your heart, and tell Father that the desire of your heart is to serve Him from now on. Ask God to save you and give your heart to Him. Then, re-read the book. And, welcome to the family! I'll see you at Home later on.

...

If you would like to contact the author about arranging speaking engagements or seminars, please visit www.bibleforlifemin.org or send an email to LvnthLrd2@msn.com.

www.ingramcontent.com/pod-product-compliance
Lightning Source LLC
Chambersburg PA
CBHW050836160426
43192CB00010B/2048